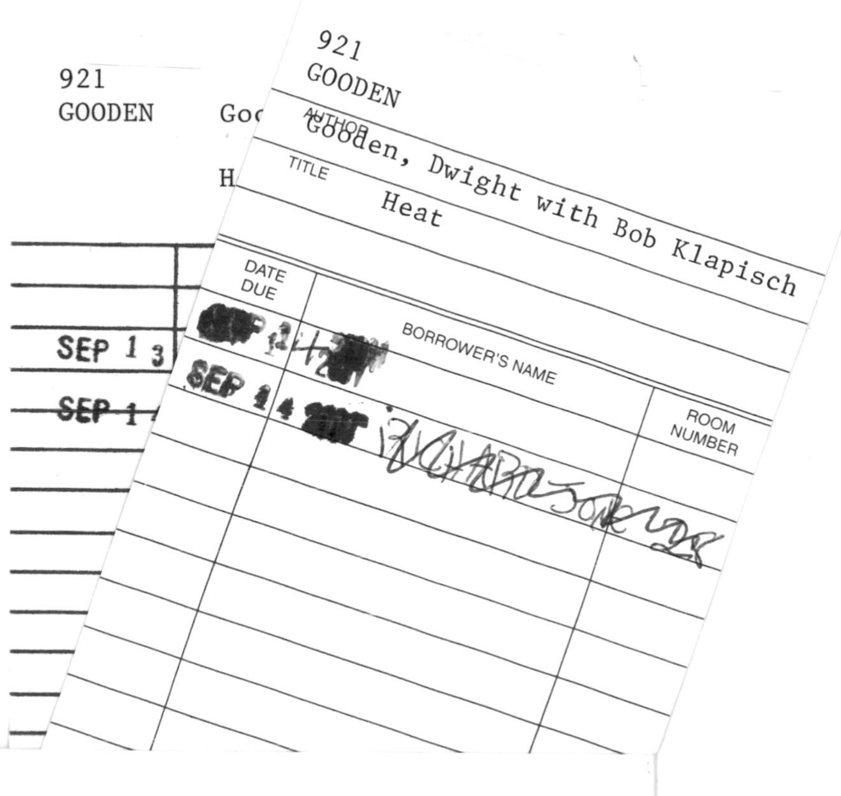


Roycemore School
MS/US Library
640 Lincoln Street
Evanston, IL 60201

# HEAT

# DWIGHT GOODEN

WITH BOB KLAPISCH

Roycemore School
MS/US Library
640 Lincoln Street
Evanston, IL 60201

# HEAT

## MY LIFE ON AND OFF THE DIAMOND

921
GOODEN

WILLIAM MORROW AND COMPANY, INC • NEW YORK

3 2001 00011720 0

Copyright © 1999 by Dwight Gooden with Bob Klapisch

The photographs in *Heat* are the property of Dwight Gooden. Reprinted by permission.

All rights reserved. No part of this book may be reproduced or utilized in any form or by any means, electronic or mechanical, including photocopying, recording, or by any information storage or retrieval system without permission in writing from the Publisher. Inquiries should be addressed to Permissions Department, William Morrow and Company, Inc., 1350 Avenue of the Americas, New York, N.Y. 10019.

It is the policy of William Morrow and Company, Inc., and its imprints and affiliates, recognizing the importance of preserving what has been written, to print the books we publish on acid-free paper, and we exert our best efforts to that end.

Library of Congress Cataloging-in-Publication data is available.

ISBN 0-688-16339-4

Printed in the United States of America

First Edition

1 2 3 4 5 6 7 8 9 10

BOOK DESIGN BY JO ANNE METSCH

www.williammorrow.com

APR 10 2001

*To my father: Still in my heart, always.*

*To my mom: The greatest.*

*To Monica: Your support can't ever be replaced.*

*To George Steinbrenner: I fell down, you picked me up. Thanks.*

# ACKNOWLEDGMENTS

This book would not have been possible without the help and inspiration of several people. First, my agent, David Vigliano, for finding a home for these words. My editor, Zach Schisgal, for his patience and wisdom. The Morris Mariners, the 30-AA Roy Hobbs World Series Champions, for their spiritual assistance during an historic week at the Royal Beach Club. And Kristy Kollar, for putting up with a crazy summer.

BK

October 1998

# FOREWORD BY

# RAY NEGRON

I REMEMBER THE day Dwight Gooden came to my home in St. Petersburg, holding his young daughter in his arms, looking for a second chance in his life. This was late in 1994, and Doc was out of baseball, and seemingly out of luck.

The players were on strike, and Doc himself had been cut loose by the Mets. He visited me because he thought I could help him find work in the Japanese baseball leagues. But after talking for only a few minutes, I could tell Dwight needed more than just a new team; he needed a new way to fight his addiction.

Until that day, Dwight had been alone in this battle—even though he'd passed through the much-respected rehabilitation programs at Smithers and Betty Ford. The doctors there gave Doc all the classroom tools an addict needs, but without a way to apply them on the street. Or in the clubhouse. Or the dangerous nightlife that can swallow up a baseball player.

I knew firsthand what drugs can do to human life. I lost a brother to AIDS, which he contracted through the use of an infected needle. His downward path started in his teens, when I caught him stealing money from our mother's purse. He begged me not to say anything, and through some foolish loyalty, I maintained my silence.

He would disappear for days and weeks, lying about his absences, and yet always returning in time to ask me for another loan. I kept giving and giving, somehow believing him that this was the last time. I should've known better.

My faith in my brother was shattered once and for all in the middle of the night seven years ago, when I received a desperation phone call. He said his car had broken down somewhere in Hudson County, New Jersey, and that he needed money for the tow.

Faithful to the end, I made the trek from the Belmont section of Queens across the Hudson River, trying to find the street address that he'd given me. I stopped dead in my tracks when I felt a pistol pressed tightly to the back of my head.

"Just give me the cash," a man said. I never saw the guy; I just handed him my wallet, too scared to turn around. Of course, I never found my brother, and to this day, I feel he set me up for that robbery.

I had my own battles with addiction, too, although not with drugs. I started gambling in the late eighties as a way of dealing with a troubled marriage. Instead of going to a scheduled counseling session one day, I kept driving and went right to Belmont Racetrack. I knew nothing about the horses, but I still managed to win $3,000 in the first five races.

That was a curse, of course—the fates' way of sucking me in. I lost all the money the very next day, and in the months that followed, proceeded to blow through my entire life savings—nearly $50,000 poured into my gambling disease. By the end, after my wife had left me, I'd become a pathetic figure. My last day at Belmont was the worst, as I wandered through the grandstands looking for someone to lend me a dollar so I could take the train home. I was completely broke, a predicament that, even today, I cannot share with my children: Jon, Erik, Toni, Joey, and Rickey.

All this made it possible for me to understand Dwight's pain. He needed help, and he needed someone to believe in him. I found the appropriate counseling services in St. Petersburg, which helped Doc apply the knowledge he'd gained from Smithers and Betty Ford. Then, through hard work, prayer, and a little luck, we helped find Dwight the baseball people with the courage to give him that second chance.

First and foremost, it was George Steinbrenner who helped Dwight rehabilitate his career. I will never forget the day Steinbrenner said to Doc, "We've all done things in this life that we regret. I'm not any different than you in that respect."

And with that, the two shook hands. Doc's career with the Yankees had begun. Although he played in the Bronx for only two years, they were hugely productive for Dwight, and set the stage for his eventual signing with the Indians.

I, too, went to Cleveland, to act as Doc's day-to-day liaison and special adviser, baseball operations. Doc pitched superbly as the Tribe won the Central Division championship in 1998, and he helped them nearly upset the Yankees in the American League Championship Series. Gooden has been drug-free for four years, and for that, Doc can thank the faith placed in him by Indians' general manager John Hart, Indians' team psychologist Charles Maher, and Louis Melendez, associate counsel of the Player Relations Committee. Also, Adelle Smithers never lost faith in difficult times.

All these people have helped Dwight find the self-confidence to face his addiction, one day at a time, which is the only way he will have a meaningful life, even after baseball.

Dwight's comeback has shown that there's no shame in admitting to a struggle with drugs. With patience and encouragement, the war can be won. That's why it's imperative that Major League Baseball institute a mandatory drug-testing program as soon as possible, to deal with this problem before it takes one more superstar. Or one more bench player. Or anyone in between.

Drugs are an equal-opportunity destroyer of lives, both on and off the field. We need all the weapons at our disposal to defeat this enemy.

Ray Negron
October 1998

# HEAT

## May 14, 1996

MY MERCEDES SL 500 had traveled about half the distance between Roslyn, Long Island, and 161st Street in the Bronx, which meant I was at the front gates of my old home, Shea Stadium. There it was, gray and desolate, more colorless than I'd ever remembered it in the eighties. Funny how time diminishes the things you once considered so huge, so important. It's like returning to your old high school, years after graduating, and realizing the hallways are smaller, the desks are tinier, the gym more compressed, and the teachers, even the toughest ones, turn out to be just regular people.

The Shea Stadium in my mind was sold-out, alive, seductive. It felt like the place was packed every night, and the Mets were communing with this living, breathing mass of people in the stands. On this day, though, Shea just looked dirty and washed-out. Still, I almost made a right turn off the Grand Central Parkway, toward the players' entrance—all by reflex. It goes to show that, even when you're in control of a car moving at sixty miles an hour, you can still be far, far away, especially if there's a crisis going on in your head.

I missed Shea—sometimes, anyway. I went past the place every day on my way to Yankee Stadium and there wasn't one instance where I didn't still feel a stab of nostalgia. So many memories from the Mets: winning the Rookie of the Year award in 1984, winning the Cy Young Award in 1985, then winning the World Series in 1986, which to me, was the greatest single accomplishment I'd been part of.

I remember how crowded the highways used to be, too, back in the days when everyone in the city was a Met fan. How driving to Shea meant that you were absolutely guaranteed to get swallowed up in some massive traffic jam. Kevin McReynolds hated the traffic so much, I swear he was already out the clubhouse door before half of us had come in from the dugout after the last out. We used to laugh about it, but in a good way, because it showed how much New York had embraced us. But in 1996, the Mets seemed dead. All the great players had moved on or retired. New Yorkers had shifted their attention to the Yankees, just like me.

There were moments where it was still impossible to believe I was wearing pinstripes. Me, a Yankee. Keith Hernandez would've killed me if he'd known ten years earlier that I'd end up in the Bronx. God, we hated the Yankees back then—their arrogance, their so-called tradition, the airs they put on that New York belonged to them, even though everyone knew the Mets were a better team.

But the Yankees had turned out to be my life preserver in 1996, when I was trying to reclaim my career and my life. As I paid the toll at the Triboro Bridge that day, crossing into the Bronx, I thought to myself: This is right, this is where I belong. I only wish that I could've enjoyed it a little more, because my mind wasn't anywhere close to the game I was supposed to pitch that night.

Normally, I focus on the opposing hitters, creating images in my head that I can take into the game. I'd drawn the Mariners, a last-minute assignment because David Cone had developed a bizarre condition in his shoulder, an aneurysm. I should've been thinking about how to deal with Ken Griffey and Jay Buhner and Edgar Martinez, but instead, my focus was back in Tampa, where my father was only twenty-four hours away from undergoing open-heart surgery.

I'd been dealing with my father's illness for almost ten years, ever since he began kidney dialysis in 1986, and it took its toll on me. It's an awful thing, watching a parent grow old and sick. It changes the way you look at yourself, makes you realize that in many ways, you're aging, too. And that scared me.

Dad's decline was so immediate, it actually took me years to accept. Suddenly my father was a prisoner of the dialysis machine, hours at a time, three days a week, and it affected the lives of everyone in the family. He needed a hip replacement in 1992, and after that came diabetes. And in January 1996 came one more setback: my dad was getting out of my grandfather's pickup truck, and just like that, the new hip was jarred out of its socket.

The doctors knew they'd have to operate on him again, but during their presurgery examinations, they realized my father urgently needed open-heart surgery. It was then, finally, that I realized my father wouldn't last much longer, although it was too painful for me to actually tell myself that. For weeks during spring training, he would make regular visits to the hospital, as they tried to build up his strength for the upcoming procedure. But one day a cardiologist at St. Joe's told my mother, "We can't wait any longer. It has to be now. In the next twenty-four hours."

My mom called me, crying like I'd never heard her cry before. "You have to come home," she said, a day before I was supposed to return to the rotation and face Seattle. I thought of the crossroads I faced: here was my chance to get back in the Yankees' good graces after I'd started the season, 0–3. Cone was on the DL and now the Yankees were leaning on me. But so was my dad.

He was a strong man, but after he'd come through that hip-replacement surgery, I remember him saying, "Dwight, I'll never make it through an operation. Never. That's my last one."

There was something about the way he looked at me when he uttered those words, as if I was hearing an unspoken request. Maybe Dad was telling me: Don't ever let me suffer, if

I can't make this decision on my own. I wish I could've asked him what he was feeling, because he was in no condition to speak, lying in that hospital bed in Tampa, with tubes running in and out of him.

After my mom had called, I went through the worst night of my life. I called the hospital every fifteen minutes, until the switchboard shut down. Since my wife, Monica, and our children were in Tampa, too, I was completely by myself in Roslyn, trying to sleep. It was pointless. I kept tossing and turning, thinking that I might never see my father again. I slept a total of forty-five minutes, so when I got up in the morning, I had this distinct buzzing in my head. I was so tired, my eye sockets literally hurt.

I wanted to be at his side, to hold his hand, tell him he'd be okay. To thank him for every single piece of advice that he ever gave me. Dad always said: "Baseball comes first. It's your dream, so live it." So I here was, living out my dream, which was really his dream, too—a former semipro first baseman whose son had made it to the big leagues at the age of nineteen.

I couldn't shake the flashbacks I had of him standing next to me on the Little League field, teaching me the fundamentals of pitching: lift your leg, stay back, keep your arm up. I remember how proud he was when I signed with the Mets, and when I finally made my first Major League start. I remember the look of devastation on his face the day I came home in 1987 and confessed that I'd tested positive for cocaine use, and how it tore him up even more when I relapsed in 1994.

Every thought I had was filled by my father. So what the hell was I doing on the northbound Major Deegan at this moment, driving that last half mile stretch to the Stadium, when my father needed me? Why didn't I just get on a plane and fly to Tampa? How could I be so selfish? Already, Joe Torre and Mel Stottlemyre had told me I had permission to be with my family. I didn't even have to ask—all I had to do was turn around and drive to La Guardia Airport. Thirty minutes, tops, and I'd be on a flight home.

George Steinbrenner had called me that morning, too, specifically to say, "If you feel you have to be in Tampa, go ahead. We understand. Our prayers are with you, Dwight." I thanked George, put down the phone, and wondered: What would my dad want?

Baseball first. Baseball first. But did that mean even when he was fighting for his life?

PART I

# EARLY DAYS

# ONE

THE KEY TO being a successful pitcher is mastering The Stare. I know that sounds strange, because you'd think getting hitters out is about throwing a ninety-plus fastball, or a neck-to-knees curveball, or having a great third pitch, like David Cone's splitter or the change-up Frank Viola used to throw in his prime.

You need all that to win. But without The Stare, you're done. The Stare comes from within—it's an attitude that tells a hitter, without words: "I'm better than you are. I'm going to get you out, and I'm going to crush your spirit in the process." You can't fake an attitude like that. If you do, you'll look like a punk. You have to believe in yourself, and that comes from your background.

I remembering hearing John Wetteland explain this phenomenon to a reporter once, and it made all the sense in the world. He said, "You can throw a fastball, as hard as you possibly can, right on a corner, right at the knees, and if you have confidence in that pitch, you're going to get a hitter out with it. But if you go into your windup thinking the catcher called for the wrong pitch—if you're not one hundred percent sure you're right about throwing it—I guarantee you that same exact pitch is going to get hit over the wall."

In a slightly different way, I learned that lesson from my father, all the way back in Little League. My father loved his brief career as a semipro player. He went on to work in a chemical plant in Tampa, but kept in touch with baseball by coaching a semipro team in the neighborhood.

My mom, Ella, was a nurse's aide; she was kind and loving at home and levelheaded about the world around us. But Dad . . . he was all about sports. He was the one who taught me how to walk and talk like a real ballplayer, and that tutoring began even before I even started playing.

Since we lived in Tampa, it wasn't too far to travel to Lakeland, where the Detroit Tigers had their spring training camp. There, we got to watch the great Al Kaline hit. He crushed a home run the very first time I saw a Tigers game, and ever since then, I was an Al Kaline fan. I was only six, but I made up my mind that I wanted to be a Major Leaguer.

Soon after, my favorite pastime was sitting next to my dad when he was in his easy chair watching the *Game of the Week* on TV. I'd have a bag of chips and a soda, and he'd be drinking a beer, and for hours I learned, just listening to Dad dissect a game.

I remember one time, when Bob Gibson was pitching, my father said, "That man isn't afraid of anyone. Look at him." And it was true, even though I was only seven, I could sense Gibson's ferocity. You just knew that no one wanted to fuck with him. He had this wild, all-arms-and-legs windup, and a three-quarters delivery that made him poison to right-handed hitters. But as I came to learn later in life, what really made Gibson a Hall of Famer is that he never surrendered the inside corner. He made it his, and wouldn't think twice about knocking a hitter down to cement that point.

I guess that's why my father admired Gibson so much, and why Gibson scared the hell out of me, even through the TV set. I wanted to be mean, just like Gibson. Trouble is, being a tough guy wasn't that easy when you were skinny, shy, and the youngest player around.

When I was seven I joined the Belmont Heights Little League, but I didn't last very long that year. For some reason, I was too embarrassed and too shy to play in front of my parents. All I ever wanted to do was stay in the dugout, because I was afraid that I wasn't good enough to please my dad. So for a couple of games, I just never showed up, and when I did, I hid behind the bats.

My coach was a friend of my father's, though—he was actually a player on the semipro team that Dad was coaching—so he urged me to come back the next year. And my father made it clear there would be no quitting again.

"I let you walk away once," he said. "But if you ever quit on baseball again, I'm not letting you play, ever again. You understand that? Baseball's not for quitters."

That was the first lesson he ever taught me about believing in myself, but I still had a long way to go. That year, when I was eight, my team finished in last place, 3–16, and every game we lost, we were blown out by ten or more runs. One more time, I told my dad that baseball wasn't any fun, and once again, I learned a lesson that I kept with me for a long time.

"Just because those kids are making errors doesn't mean that you should quit on them," he said. "They're doing the best they can with the skills they have, which is all I'm ever going to ask of you. Just be able to look in the mirror and say, 'I gave a hundred percent,' and you'll be able to live with yourself."

I was rushed along in the Little League, moved up to the eleven-

and twelve-year-old division, even though I was only ten. My dad was this team's coach, and I guess he saw something in me, although at that age, I was still small and skinny and shy, scared half out of my mind all the time. Playing with the older kids was a huge trauma, especially since I was asked to be a third baseman.

I couldn't believe how hard these kids threw the ball, and how quickly the ball came off their bats. I was in way over my head. I went 0 for 5 on opening day, striking out three times. Which is another way of saying I was a total failure, despite all my father's efforts to coach me along.

Even worse, I was expected to hit off this kid Albert Everett, whose brother Carl went on to play for the Mets. Everett threw so hard, I saw him break a kid's cheekbone with a fastball. I wanted out. I didn't want anything to do with the bigger kids.

I wanted to go back to the Minor League division and play with the younger kids again. That's where I felt more comfortable, but this is where my father drew the line. He and my coach said, "You're staying in the Major League."

So I stayed. And finally, something clicked. Don't ask me how or why, but my talent started to develop. In fact, I played a pretty decent third base, and it turned out to be a magical year. We were the 1975 national Little League champs, and we went all the way to Williamsport, Pennsylvania, for the World Series. We lost to Taiwan, and I didn't get to play, because, according to the rules, you had to be at least eleven. But it was a great experience and led me to better times in baseball.

That's because I started to grow at the age of eleven, and by the time I was twelve, I started to pitch. I'd had a hint that my arm was strong in the last year and a half, especially in throwing the ball across the diamond from third base. But pitching was a different and wonderful sensation. That's when I realized that I had a gift for throwing a ball harder than the other kids. There was one game I pitched in 1977 when I struck out sixteen, and I felt that wonderful rush a pitcher gets when he can dominate a hitter.

Even at that age, I knew that throwing a fastball, right down the middle, right by a hitter, is the reason pitchers fall in love with baseball. It's like throwing a fifty-yard TD pass, or delivering a knockout punch, or hitting a home run five hundred feet. Everything else about pitching is designed around finesse or trickery—nibbling a corner, or throwing a curveball that has a massive arc. Those are nice weapons, but nothing beats a good fastball.

Naturally, I progressed pretty fast through Little League, the Senior League division, all the way to Hillsborough HS. There's a pretty rich baseball tradition among Tampa's high schools. Among the players who went on to play in the big leagues were Wade Boggs, Tino Martinez, Fred McGriff, Steve Garvey, and Lou Piniella.

They'd all been coached by Billy Reed, who was practically a legend around Tampa. But I quickly found out what a tough, disciplined man he was, and that he intended to make an example out of me. Truth was, I was spoiled by my parents, by my dad especially, and I was growing up soft. I was by far the youngest child in the family—I had three brothers and two sisters, ranging from ten to eighteen years older than me—and I never had any chores around the house. I was the baby.

The ones that were assigned to me, like mowing the lawn, or taking out the garbage, washing the car, folding clothes, were inevitably handled by my dad. "Just go outside for a couple of hours, and when you come back, I'll say you took care of it," my father would say, winking.

Part of the reason was that my father was intent on furthering my career. Right before school would end every summer, my mom would bring home job applications, just so I could stay busy and learn something about earning and managing money. There was a Denny's restaurant opening nearby, and Mom thought it'd be a good idea for me to work there.

My father wouldn't hear of it. He'd tell her, "Dwight isn't going to be taking any job. He's going to be playing baseball this summer. He's going to be a big-league ballplayer."

Of course, Mom would roll her eyes, because she'd been hearing that since I was about eight.

"There's more to life than baseball," she'd say. "Dwight better start thinking about an education."

Actually, my mother was a lot tougher than Dad. I remember one day, just before the start of my junior year, I asked her if I could go hang out with some friends who'd congregated near the skating rink. She said no, that school was starting the next day and that she wanted me home. That was it, end of discussion. Or so she thought.

Instead of listening, I snuck out the back window, thinking I'd fooled her. But my nephew Gary Sheffield, my sister Betty's son, came by a few minutes later and said, matter-of-factly, "Your mom says next time you want to leave the house, you might as well use the front door."

She knew! How is that mothers always know? My heart started beating so fast, I thought I'd have a coronary right there in public. Five minutes later my mom drove right up to the rink. "There's your mom," I heard one of my buddies say, and I could see the rage in her face. In full view of my friends, she walked up to me and pulled me back to the car. I was humiliated, but she was out to make a point. The moment she closed the driver's-side door, she slapped me right across the head and said, "Don't you ever disrespect me again."

When we got home, she took a belt strap to me and gave me the beating of my life. I'll never forget how much that hurt, and how embarrassed I was in front of my friends the next day. Of course, Mom told Dad about it, but he never hit me. Not once.

In hindsight, I know my mother was just trying to keep me in line. She wanted me to have fun playing ball and hanging out with my friends, but her real vision of my future was to go to college, get a job, get married, start a family, and lead a respectable life.

I understood that, but my mom didn't really appreciate my gifts as a ballplayer. That's one reason why the only job I ever had—the only money I ever brought home before signing with the Mets—was cutting avocados off trees, collecting them in baskets, and then selling them in the parking lot of the grocery store around the corner. My friends and I would wait for shoppers to leave the store, and then we'd offer the avocados. We actually sold a few, which meant on the good days, I'd come home with two or three dollars.

So I guess it's fair to say I never struggled in my teens, which is why the treatment I got from Coach Reed was so shocking. I think what motivated him was the fact that Hillsborough HS had never had a star black player and Reed, who's also black, wanted to show that he wasn't going to play favorites.

In my sophomore year, for instance, Reed made me pitch batting practice, but never allowed me to hit. In the intrasquad games, he forced me to play the field for both teams and, again, prohibited me from batting. For some reason, I felt like he was punishing me, maybe because I was black, maybe because I was one of the youngest kids. To this day, I still don't know.

I was only fifteen and still eligible for the Senior League division, where I used to dominate. My dad was still coaching there, so I decided I'd had enough humiliation and aggravation and quit the Hillsborough team. I remember what my father had said about quitting, but this time he agreed that Reed had gone too far, and welcomed me back.

Reed was furious. He told another coach, "Gooden just wants to play with the little kids. Let him go. That's where he belongs." In fact, he sent word that I would never be allowed back on the high-school team. Now I was really mad, knowing that he was bad-mouthing me. So with my parents' permission, I was planning to move in with my sister Mercedes across town, which would've made me eligible to play for Robertson HS, a longtime rival of Hillsborough's.

The coach at Robertson was Dave Best, who had a pretty good program of his own. I let friends on the Hillsborough team know that if I played for Robertson, I'd make a point of pitching against Hillsborough and not just beat them, but smother them. I guess that's what my father meant all along about attitude. I was starting to develop it—enough so that I forced Reed into backing down.

He did eventually relent, asking me back on the Hillsborough team. I agreed. Actually, I was thrilled. But Reed had to have the last word. He made me play in the school's winter league, including practicing with the freshmen and sophomores and players changing to new positions, all during the Christmas vacation. I suppose I needed the discipline, but at age fifteen it's hard to see it that way.

I mean, this was worse than having a strict father. It was like having a twenty-four-hour-a-day drill sergeant looking over your shoulder. Just before the season opener in my junior year, Reed found out that I'd been late for home room, by just a little bit. Still, he took the opportunity to bench me for that day's game, even though I'd won the job as the starting right fielder and had invited a girl I was trying to impress.

That's the funny thing about my high-school career. As much as I'd dominated as a pitcher in Little League and the Senior League, I wasn't really pursuing pitching in my teens. I loved hitting so much, plus the inning-by-inning action I got as a position player. In fact, if it hadn't been for a dispute my teammate and friend Floyd Youmans had with Coach Reed, it's possible my career in baseball would never have included pitching.

Floyd was a terrific athlete, and he went on to have a brief career in the big leagues with the Phillies and Expos in the mid-1980s. He could throw as hard as anyone I ever saw, harder than me, in fact, and if it weren't for a drug problem that he succumbed to as a Major Leaguer, I have no doubt Floyd would've still been playing today.

Trouble was, Floyd always had a problem with authority back then. I guess we all did, but he made the mistake of lying to Coach Reed one day, and got caught. Floyd asked if he could leave practice early because of some baby-sitting responsibilities. Reed said okay, but he had this amazing BS detector and knew Floyd had other plans. Coach left practice a few minutes after Floyd, and, naturally, found him playing basketball with a couple of buddies. Reed kicked Floyd off the team and moved me right into the rotation.

Until that point the best I could've hoped for was a few relief appearances, but suddenly I became one of Hillsborough's most important starters. I went 7–0 that year with a 0.76 ERA, and in one game I pitched during the Easter tournament, I threw a one-hitter, facing the minimum twenty-one batters. The only guy who singled was immediately thrown out trying to steal second, and because of that game, I was named the tournament Most Valuable Player. That summer I played American League ball, and I started to pile up the strikeouts in a steady blur.

That was also the time when Julius Erving still had a hold on the basketball public, and his nickname, Dr. J., stuck. One day out of the stands, when I had two strikes on a hitter I knew didn't have a chance on my next fastball, I heard a fan yell out, "Go get him, Dwight. Operate on him, Doc." Other people in the stands must've heard the nickname and liked it, because from that day forward, fans started referring to me as Doctor. Eventually, I was known as just Doc.

My senior year, Floyd moved to California and I was the only experienced pitcher on Hillsborough's team. It was a rebuilding season for us, so I hardly dominated. In fact, I was only 7–4, although I did have a 1.30 ERA, and struck out 130 in seventy-five innings. I had a good year as a hitter, too, batting .340 and playing third base on the days I wasn't pitching.

I was a little surprised to discover that I was being scouted. I mean, I knew it was easy for me to pile up the strikeouts, but I wasn't the best pitcher in the area. Both Rich Monteleone and Lance McCullers were the standouts, and both went on to have careers in the big leagues. In fact, the scouts that did pay attention to me seemed to think of me as a position player, and not as a pitcher.

I think they saw me merely as a strong-armed athlete who could easily be converted into a third baseman or right fielder. What the scouts didn't realize was that I'd pitched in almost two thirds of Hillsborough's games that season, and there were many instances where I just didn't have my best stuff.

The reason for that was our schedule, which called for us to play on Tuesdays, Fridays, and Saturdays. I'd normally start on Tuesday, then play third base or right field on Friday night, and then start again on Saturday morning. And sometimes, if it was a close game on Friday, I'd come in relief. More than once that season, I pitched three times in a week, but no one seemed to realize that. No one, except the Mets.

I never really thought about a professional career going beyond Class A or Double A. I knew I'd been able to dominate the kids in the Tampa area, but I lacked the self-confidence to realize that I could play at any level. The Mets thought otherwise, making me their first round of the 1982 amateur draft.

I was stunned, actually, to learn I was the fifth pick in the entire nation. McCullers and Monteleone were selected ahead of me, as was Shawon Dunston, a shortstop, and Jimmy Jones, another right-hander. But I was sure that the announcement of my selection was a hoax as it appeared on the wire. I'd been invited by the editors of *The Tampa Tribune* to witness the draft from their offices, which was a nice story idea. But I wasn't buying into the fact that the Mets picked me, not until those newspaper people called New York and verified it.

I didn't know much about the Mets, but it sure looked like I was going to be playing for them. I'd already signed a letter of intent with the University of Miami, mostly out of deference to my mom, but everyone in the family agreed that if I was picked by any team in the first five rounds, I'd give pro ball a shot.

I remember the man who came to the house to sign me. His name was Joe McIlvaine, a tall, easygoing man who knew his baseball. Of all the scouts who'd watched me play at Hillsborough, he was the only who was aware of my overloaded pitching schedule. I read later in the newspaper that McIlvaine said, "No one knew how good Dwight really was."

That was nice to hear, but now it was McIlvaine's job to bring me into the Met family at the cheapest possible price. That was business' role reversal: from liking me enough to draft me, to trying to squeeze me out of a few bucks. I didn't really have an agent yet, so I let my father act as the go-between. And for all the coddling and soft treatment I received from my dad growing up, I got a firsthand look at just how tough he could be.

When McIlvaine offered $40,000 as a signing bonus, my father told him not to waste our time. We were all sitting in the living room, and I nearly passed out. That was $40,000 my dad just said no to. God, I would've accepted $1,000! That's why I don't understand some of these rookies, like J. D. Drew, who are holding out for more and more money and creating an enormous backlash against themselves.

Drew, backed up by his super-tough agent, Scott Boras, went so far as to sit out for a year when they couldn't come to terms with the Phillies in 1997 after demanding $11 million up front. I understand Drew's a pretty talented hitter and will undoubtedly prosper on the major league level. But still, to ask for that much cash without ever having played an inning in the big leagues, that was too rich for my blood. Drew actually gave up an entire summer playing in the Northern League, and then reentered the draft and eventually signed with the Cardinals.

But that's not to say there's anything wrong with negotiating, because my dad sure played it tough with McIlvaine. After turning down $40,000, the Mets eventually raised their offer to $70,000. I remember distinctly how McIlvaine sat in front of me, my mom, and my dad and said it was the best the club could do.

"If you're looking for more than that, I'm afraid we're going to have to bow out," McIlvaine said politely.

My father looked Joe Mac straight in the eye and said, "Then I'm sorry, sir. But we're at the end of the road."

There was an awful silence in the room. I didn't realize at the time that these two men were just playing poker. I was scared that my career was over before it'd even started, and that I'd either end up playing for Miami, which I didn't really want to do, or else I'd be flipping burgers at Denny's, after all.

McIlvaine got up from the couch, shook my father's hand, and as he prepared to walk out the door, said to me, "Good luck, son."

That was pure pain, watching Joe leave. I literally had to stop myself from chasing him out to the driveway, before he got to his car and drove off. I wanted stop McIlvaine and say, "Yes, I'll take the $70,000." But I didn't do that. I waited until McIlvaine was gone and then looked at my father, my face a blend of disbelief and fear and rage.

"How could you say no, Dad? They're offering us great money. I'll take it right now," I said. My father just looked right back at me, his voice calm as always. That man had no fear.

"They'll be back," Dad said finally. "They know how good you are. And believe me, son, they'll respect you more that you held out."

He was right, of course. My dad usually was. A few days later

McIlvaine called back and agreed to pay us $85,000, although my father said I wouldn't be allowed to spend the money until after the season. That meant no car—I'd already picked out a brand-new, silver Camaro Z28—no new clothes, nothing, until I'd finished a season in rookie ball.

"Now it's time to get to work," he said. "You've waited for this for a long, long time. You're going to make the most of it."

THERE WAS A week's lapse between the time we signed all the contracts and when I was supposed to report to Kingsport, where the Mets Rookie League team played. There were celebration parties, farewell parties, a lot of hugging and kidding and crying. But I have to admit, when the day came for me to leave home, I was close to tears.

I'd never really spent any time away from my mother and father, except for the two weeks when I went to Williamsport, Pennsylvania, for the Little League World Series. The Mets bought me a first-class ticket to fly to Kingsport, and even before the plane landed, I was already homesick.

I must've called my parents seven times that very first day, and after that, at least ten times a week. I called because I didn't know how to cook, how to wash my own clothes, or fold my laundry. I called because I didn't know how to shop for food, or to open a bank account.

My mom was worried enough that pretty soon I started eating TV dinners, just so that I could tell her I was eating. My dad wasn't so sympathetic. In fact, after my third call of the day one time, he took the phone away from my mom and said, "Stop calling here so much. Start acting like a grown-up. You can call once or twice a week, but that's it."

That was the first time my dad had ever spoken so harshly to me. That, combined with the homesickness and the fact that I was only 5–4 with a 2.57 ERA, made pro baseball seem less fun than I'd imagined. I didn't really know anyone, and the team was pretty lousy. At one point we lost sixteen in a row, and there were days when I missed home so bad, I considered just getting on a bus and leaving.

My year away from my parents wasn't made any easier by the fact that in early August, the Mets promoted me to Little Falls, New York, near Utica, in the New York–Penn League. That was also a Rookie League, but a slightly higher level of competition. It was like starting all over, with teammates I'd never met before.

I also found it slightly uncomfortable to be one of only two black players on the roster. The other was Johnny Wilson, the younger brother of outfielder Mookie Wilson. Although there were no racial problems on the team itself, being isolated in this way was just another thing I had to get used to. The town of Little Falls was all-white, too, and whenever I went out with guys on the team for dinner or a beer or two, people stared at me.

I called my parents and told them that I was uncomfortable with my surroundings, that while the players were fine, the racial overtones in the town were uglier than I'd anticipated. This time my father knew I wasn't talking about homesickness. He knew it was a serious matter and suggested I speak to my manager, Sam Perlozzo.

The only problem was my own shyness. I was barely able to talk to my teammates in the dugout during games. How was I going to address an issue so sensitive as racial epithets? I thought of a way I could speak to Perlozzo without looking like a baby, or someone who is overfocused on racial issues.

But I couldn't. I decided to let the matter drop and just finish out the season. By the time I got home in late summer, I was ready for some time off. So was my arm. For the first time in my life I experienced shoulder fatigue, which the Mets doctor said was a mild case of tendinitis, probably from all the innings I'd thrown that year, in high school, at Kingsport and then at Little Falls. By the spring of 1983, the Mets sent me to Lynchburg, which was their highest level of Class A ball.

Obviously, the franchise had plans for me. Big plans. But I started the season just as I ended at rookie ball—with a mediocre record, barely over .500. I never told anyone, but I was just happy to win a few more games than I lost, happy not to embarrass myself, just to keep my head above water. In other words, I wanted to be invisible.

The team's pitching instructors clocked my fastball at ninety-two miles an hour, which is well above the major league average. But I had the mentality of a journeyman: with a 3–2 record, I was going nowhere. I forget who it was I was pitching against, but one day I was down 2–0 in the second inning with the bases loaded and no one out. That's when John Cumberland, the pitching coach at Lynchburg, came to the mound.

Most of the time pitching coaches visit you just to make small talk, just to give you a chance to collect your thoughts, almost like a battered fighter getting that sixty-second break between rounds. Very rarely will there be any actual instruction or technical advice; it's all about psychology.

Which is exactly why Cumberland was now standing inches from my face.

"Let me ask you something, son," Cumberland said. Before I could open my mouth, he shouted, *"What the fuck is your problem?"*

I was so stunned, I couldn't even begin to speak, which was fine with Cumberland. This wasn't about to be a two-way discussion.

"You've got one of the best arms I've ever seen on a kid, and you're pitching like you've got no balls. None at all. Fuck, you keep throwing like that, you might as well pack up and get the fuck home. I'm one of the few people in the fucking organization that still believes in you, but personally, I don't think you've got it in you. You hearing me?"

I nodded. What else could I do? Cumberland was a former major league pitcher who I respected. He'd won his share of games with the Giants, but more than that, you could tell he was fearless. He had a hard face, one whose features said: Don't Ever Fuck with Me.

I wasn't about to.

"Now, I want you to get out of this inning. I want you to shove the ball down their throats, because you've got the skill to do it, son. Show me you've got the stones."

With that, Cumberland walked off the mound and returned to the dugout. Everyone has a defining moment in his career; looking back, that verbal flogging I took from Cumberland was mine. Something inside me just snapped. I was so embarrassed at the way he spoke to me in front of everyone—teammates, opposing players, umpires, even the fans were able to hear him—I was beyond shame.

I took a deep breath, went into my windup, and struck out the side in eleven pitches. Don't ask me where the rage came from, but for the first time in my life I was pitching with an attitude. It's like my dad had taught me all along: you can't break out The Stare unless, somewhere deep inside of you, you're telling the hitter I'm better than you.

Suddenly I knew I was. I finished the 1983 season with a 19–4 record, a 2.50 ERA, and three hundred strikeouts in just 191 innings. The Mets decided I didn't need any more tutoring. I skipped Double A and Triple A and by the spring of 1984, I was on my way to New York.

# TWO

EVEN TODAY, MORE than a decade later, I get goose bumps watching films of myself pitching in 1984 and 1985. I had that massive leg kick back then, a chaotic delivery that I knew made it impossible for hitters to pick up the ball. That, and the fact that my fastball seemed to grow muscles all by itself between '83 and '84.

I wish I could've appreciated how quickly I burst onto the National League in my rookie year, but I couldn't. Everything happened so damned fast. I remember telling my father in spring training that I'd be happy just being a .500 pitcher, and the next thing I knew, I was chasing Herb Score's old record for the most strikeouts by a rookie pitcher.

I never ever thought I would be that good, that early in my career. Hell, I didn't even know anything about the old-timer whose record I was breaking. I had to ask the Mets trainer, Steve

Garland, all about Score so I would sound halfway intelligent when the press asked me about him. Truth was, I was still a terribly shy kid who, away from the ballpark, out of the spotlight, was happy just sitting at home watching TV or playing video games.

I might've gotten away with that lifestyle had I played for a small-market team, but I found myself not only in the most overheated sports environment in the country, but in a clubhouse with some very young, very talented, very cocky players.

My orientation to the Mets began the day I met Darryl Strawberry in spring training. Naturally, I'd heard about him when I was at Lynchburg. Everyone had. He had that long, beautiful swing, the funny name, and as much talent as any hitter I'd ever seen. Little did I know that Straw had a major league presence about him that I found to be close to intimidating.

The first time we met was in the outfield at Miller Huggins Field, where the Mets used to have their spring training. Darryl was cool and laid-back. You could tell he had a street sense about him. I came from a much different background—softer, more coddled, less challenging. I guess Straw saw that right away.

"You know what your problem is, Doc?" he said. "You don't look like a big-leaguer ballplayer. You don't talk like one. Man, you don't even walk like one." I asked him what he meant.

"Look at you. You got your head down all the time like you're embarrassed to be here. You can't even look anyone in the eye. I've seen you. I know how good you are. You just don't know it yet." I couldn't believe that my shyness was so obvious to the rest of the world. Strawberry was right, of course.

I'd mastered The Stare in the Minor Leagues, but now that I was surrounded by Major Leaguers, some doubts crept back. So that night I went home and checked myself out in the mirror. I walked, straight and tough, the way Straw suggested. I practiced looking mean. I practiced rolling my shoulders. I even developed an arrogant way of spitting.

I made up my mind that night that no one was going to take advantage of me. I had a great fastball, a great gift, and I wasn't going to waste it.

Still, there were lessons to learn on the field. In my rookie year, I remember getting lit up by the Cubs, who in 1984 were our primary rivals in the East. We'd won six of our first seven games in April, including my first career victory, when I beat the Astros in the Dome. Now I was facing the Cubs in Wrigley Field, and I found out what a burden it can be to be a hotshot rookie.

They scored a run on me in the first inning, and stayed all over me, scoring six runs by the fourth. I didn't have much of a fastball, and it sure didn't help that Wrigley had such a flat mound. Everything I threw was up, and the more I tried to compensate, the longer and uglier my delivery became. That only made it easier for the Cubs to steal bases on my catcher, John Gibbons.

By the fourth, I was history, and I was so embarrassed when Davey Johnson came to get me, I didn't even wait for Ed Lynch to come in from the bullpen. I practically sprinted back to the dugout. Still, I did manage to see the Cubs were high-fiving each other like crazy, as if they'd just won the World Series. The final was 11–2, and what they were really happy about, of course, was seeing a rookie having his lunch handed to him. After the game I told a reporter I didn't appreciate the way the Cubs were celebrating.

Somehow, my words were misconstrued, and it appeared in the next day's paper that I'd called the Cubs "hot dogs." I'm sure they were ticked off at me. There's no greater common enemy in the big leagues than a loudmouthed rookie. That's why their shortstop, Larry Bowa, approached me at the batting cage and asked me if the quote was accurate.

"No, I didn't say that exactly," I told Bowa.

"We figured that," he said. "You gotta watch what you say to the press. Most of the time you'll get fucked."

I never had a problem with the press in New York, despite this one miscommunication. On the whole, I like the reporters who covered the Mets in the eighties—Danny Castellano from the Newark Star-*Ledger*, Joe Durso from *The New York Times*, and Tom Verducci, who was then at *Newsday* and now is at *Sports Illustrated*, were all straight with me.

So I was willing to let one misquote go by. My real problem was with the Cubs, and what I should've told Bowa was, whether I used the term "hot dog" or not, I didn't appreciate the way he and his teammates behaved. It all went back to Straw's lesson—that part of being a Major Leaguer was acting like one, and it angered me that the Cubs thought they could get away with such disrespect.

But I'm usually not an in-your-face kind of guy—not now, and certainly not then, in 1984. I walked away from Bowa, vowing to exact my revenge the old-fashioned way, by throwing unhittable fastballs the next time I faced them. Fortunately, we got the Cubs on the very next homestand, and even luckier for me, I was scheduled to pitch the opening game of that series.

To say that I was pumped up is an understatement. Pumped up, and with even more confidence than my Wrigley start, because after losing to the Cubs, I beat the Reds and the Expos, and I even got to face one of my idols, Pete Rose. I remember just before my first pitch to Rose, Keith Hernandez came over to me and said, "Don't be nervous, Doc. His bat's not as quick as it used to be. Just work him in, he won't catch up to you."

To my utter amazement, Hernandez was right—as he was about almost everything. I got Rose to bounce out to short, and I remember as he crossed over the infield on his way back to the dugout, I just stared at the guy. I was in total awe of his accomplishments, but also of my own ability to retire him.

I took that confidence booster with me into the Cubs game and, for seven innings, made them regret every single high five they pounded out against me two weeks earlier. In seven innings, I struck out ten, allowed just four hits, and walked away with a one-sided 8–1 victory. That was the last time the Cubs ever tried to show me up. As a matter of fact, word spread pretty quickly in the National League that I was to be taken seriously, just like the Mets themselves.

After so many years of bad baseball, the Mets had finally arrived, and even though we finished a close second to the Cubs in '84, we were at the doorstep of a seven-year golden era at Shea.

JUST WHAT WAS my profound memory with the Mets? It wasn't any one year or game or even one player, although I maintain that, in his prime and properly motivated, Darryl Strawberry was the best hitter I saw in the eighties.

Some days, you could just tell Straw was ready to play: his eyes were clear, he looked happy, and obviously wasn't hung over. He'd say to me, "Watch me, Doc, I'm gonna hit one out today." And he would. It was that easy for him. Occasionally, Darryl would say, "Doc, I'm going to hit two." And he would.

Until 1990, I'd say Darryl was better than Ken Griffey or Barry Bonds—at least he had the potential to be. But like me, Straw robbed his career of years of excellence and cost himself a chance for the Hall of Fame. I'm glad he finally found himself by 1996, but the way he still hits HRs as a Yankee, it only makes me wonder how many more Darryl would've hit had he remained clean and sober.

But Darryl's distractions were overwhelming to him, as were mine. For all the street smarts he had growing up in South-Central L.A.: he still couldn't handle being young, suddenly very rich, and thrust into the limelight in New York. Nothing in his background could've prepared him for that.

Nobody ever told Darryl to watch out for the "friends" he was suddenly making, or that it's a cold truth that while heavy drinking can create the appearance of a good time, it destroys your reflexes. Or that money is nice, but it's not everything, and it sure doesn't last forever.

Darryl also had terrible troubles at home, which he brought with him to the ballpark. Back then, we lived near each other in Port Washington, and we'd ride together to the ballpark. I could always tell when Straw had just been in a fight with his wife, Lisa, because he usually wouldn't say a word during the entire drive. He'd just be totally within himself, obviously still replaying the argument in his head. Straw wasn't happy, and he and Lisa went through an ugly divorce in the early nineties.

Thing was, if Darryl was hung over and fighting with Lisa, he just wouldn't play. That's why Hernandez and Davey were always so angry with Darryl, just because he would give away entire games to his off-the-field distractions. He'd just walk into the trainer's room, collapse on the table and, through Steve Garland, tell Davey he wasn't playing. Lots of times, Davey would pencil Darryl in, for the simple reason that he didn't want any player making out the lineup card. And I understood that.

But I was also aware that he and Lisa were literally destroying each other. One time when I was driving Straw to the park, he was still so angry that, just a half mile from Shea, he said, "Doc, turn around, I'm going back home."

I looked at him like he was crazy.

"Straw, we're here, we got a game in a few hours," I said.

"I don't care, take me back," he said. "I ain't finished with her."

I knew there was no dissuading him, so I said, "Listen, man, I'm going into the clubhouse. You want to go home, I'll give you the car. You drive yourself back."

And he did.

That's the way the Mets existed back then: no one—not other teams, not even our own wives—messed with us. Actually, what

I'll remember most about those great Met teams was the closeness between the players. It's an old cliché in baseball that chemistry wins games. It's not always true—look at the A's in the early seventies, the Yankees in the late seventies—but in our case, it sure helped. That's because everyone in the National League hated us.

The Mets stuck together because we had no other friends. We were the biggest, the baddest, the hippest of the hip. We were good and we knew it. We stayed out late, drank, chased women, and then, in later years, in darker times, too many of us started relying on amphetamines and drugs to get by. We had plenty of fun in the eighties, which is what that decade was all about. Excess. In retrospect, though, I wish we'd paid a little more attention to the winning, and concentrated less on the partying.

I mean, everyone remembers the '86 World Series, but that's about it. We should've won the pennant at least two other years—in '85, when the Cardinals just edged us out, and again in '88, when I thought we had the most talented team in the league. I still can't forget losing to the Dodgers in the play-offs and how awful that plane ride was, coming home from L.A. after Game Seven.

For me, there will never be another year like 1985, when I was 24–4 with a 1.53 ERA. I led the NL in wins, strikeouts (268), and ERA and lost only one game after May 25. I was the youngest player to ever win the Cy Young Award, and by 1986, the only pitcher since 1900 to have two hundred strikeouts in each of his first three seasons.

Life was good. I could throw the ball by anyone, challenge them all, pour one fastball after another over the middle of the plate. And you know what? No one hit me. Every batter, it seemed, was behind in the count, 0–2. All Gary Carter had to do was put down No. 1—the fastball—and I took care of the rest. I didn't worry about location or changing speeds or any of the secondary factors of pitching. I was Doctor K, operating on National League hitters without even breaking a sweat. My fastball rose so much, I swear there were times that I'd throw it at a hitter's belt level, and by the time he'd finished swinging, the ball was around his eyes.

That was a gift, I knew. There's no way a pitching coach can teach you to make a fastball explode like that at the last moment; either you have or you don't. Nolan Ryan did. J. R. Richard did. I saw Mariano Rivera do that to hitters in 1996, but only that year. Not since. That's what's so mystifying about the art of pitching. So much of it comes from an unseen power. I mean, I had that great heater in 1985—sometimes close to ninety-six miles per hour—but that impossible-to-track, impossible-to-time movement deserted me in 1986, and never ever returned.

I know now it was the drinking that destroyed my fastball. There's no way you can keep putting alcohol into your system without it eventually slowing your reflexes. I felt the same; I mean, the ball felt small and perfect when it left my hand. But that little piece of magic I had was forever gone.

Oh, I still had velocity. Even today, I can still bring it at ninety-two mph. But I look at films of myself from 1985 and think: Was that really me? How did I do that? I was so . . . invincible. That was really the word. Bulletproof. I was like all the other Mets—Keith Hernandez, Lenny Dykstra, Ron Darling, Wally Backman, and, of course, Straw—who believed the world was theirs.

Maybe that's why I started drinking that year. I did so for two reasons. First, because everyone else on the team was getting loaded all the time, and second, because drinking allowed me to be the real me. I know that sounds strange—that for many people, alcohol is an escape from one's self. But I was being portrayed by the Mets and the media as the shy, meek, friendly kid from Tampa.

To a degree that was true, but no one knew that I had opinions and feelings, and sometimes a wild side. All those facets of my personality were locked inside. I kept them there because I didn't want to disappoint my bosses, Fred Wilpon and Nelson Doubleday. I wanted Frank Cashen, the Mets general manager, to think I was a good guy. And I never wanted to leave Jay Horwitz, the Mets public-relations director, hanging, even though sometimes there'd be six or seven camera crews waiting at my locker, each one expecting a separate one-on-one interview.

Sometimes I would be tired, dead tired. But Jay would say, "Doc, do this one for me, okay?" And I would say yes, because I liked Jay. I loved the man. He was the hardest-working, most loyal Met employee I ever saw. But I was losing myself to the media. I was becoming less and less of a person, and more and more of an image—something not real.

I was the perfect marketing tool for the Mets, because I was nonthreatening. I smiled, signed autographs, made charity appearances, played the good cop to Darryl's bad-cop persona. Trouble was, I didn't want to be a role model. I didn't ask for it, and I didn't want it. But there weren't many other choices, especially among minority Mets.

Darryl? He was too volatile and Mookie couldn't last forever in New York. Our ranks were so thin through the eighties, there were times it felt like the Mets limited the number of black players on their roster. While there was no racial tension in our clubhouse—and I mean, absolutely none—the front office somehow never assembled more than a few black athletes at any one time.

In my rookie year, the only black players were me, Straw, Hubie Brooks, George Foster, and Mookie. The club traded Hubie in 1985, then got rid of Foster, who was leading the team in home runs in 1986, because he said the Mets made certain decisions based on race. The statements caused such a commotion, everyone got hurt. George was out of a job, and we lost our most productive hitter at the time.

Was Foster right? I didn't think Mets executives were racists, but there were little things that caught my attention over the years. Like, Lenny Dykstra, who is white, and not Terry Blocker, who is black, being called up to replace Mookie after a spring-training injury in 1985. And first baseman Randy Milligan lingering in the minors, even after he'd won the International League's Triple Crown award, because Keith Hernandez didn't need a backup.

That was probably true—but the Mets did allow John Christensen, who is white, to make the team as backup outfielder. And then Rusty Tillman, another qualified black outfielder, was passed over in 1984, so Jerry Martin, a personal friend of Davey Johnson's, could make the team.

Thankfully, things are different with today's Mets. They're run by a progressive and open-minded administration, and I respect the attitudes of Steve Phillips, the general manager, and Bobby Valentine, the manager.

But being an out-front guy wasn't so easy then, especially for me. I guess that's why I felt this enormous pressure to conform to the Mets' vision of me. I had to be Mr. Everything: athlete, ambassador, marketing specialist, and all-around nice guy. The drinking was my refuge. Once I drank, I could drop the mask I was supposed to wear 24/7 and finally go to clubs with my teammates, especially on the road. Listen to music, talk to women, speak my mind. Even laugh.

Drinking allowed me to commune with Darryl and Kevin Mitchell, who was a funny, but very wild and sometimes very dangerous guy. I liked Mitch, but I knew better than to ever fuck with him. I'd heard stories about his background in San Diego, some of which included rumors that he'd hurt some people in gang-related violence. I don't know about that, but I got to witness, firsthand, Mitch's temper.

He was so good with his fists, I saw him beat up Strawberry during a pickup basketball game in spring training. Darryl liked to think he was a pretty good hoops player, and actually he was. But one day in St. Petersburg, he and Mitch were on the same team and they got into an argument about who was taking too many shots and who wasn't passing the ball. The usual stuff.

Out of nowhere, bam, Mitch slugged Darryl right in the face. Then he hit him again and knocked Straw down. It took a couple of us to pull him off, and I swear I never saw a punch that connected so cleanly. As much as I hated to see it, Mitch really did beat the hell out of Darryl.

Later that year, in 1986, we were in the middle of a bench-clearing brawl with the Pirates, and amid all the mini-fights, I saw Mitch overpower Pittsburgh's shortstop Sammy Khalifa. He took Khalifa down, got on top of him, and applied a choke hold. I couldn't believe my eyes, because Mitch was doing more than just trying to beat up Khalifa; he was attempting to kill him.

Indeed, Khalifa's eyes were wide and unseeing, and it suddenly occurred to me that he was being strangled to death. Several players, including a few Mets who saw what was going on, pulled Mitch off him. What was so scary is that later on, when we asked why the hell he wanted to kill Khalifa, Mitch couldn't remember anything about the fight.

Mitch wasn't averse to taking on even me. Later on that summer, I dropped by his house along with Meade Chassky, a card-show-and-events entrepreneur with whom I became good friends over the years. Meade and I had had lunch at my house, and we decided to pay Mitch an unannounced visit. That was a mistake.

When we got there, I realized Kevin was both drunk and angry, a dangerous combination. He was holding a twelve-inch knife in his hands, having an argument with his live-in girlfriend. Kevin was right in the girl's face, screaming at the top of his lungs.

"I told you not to fuck with me, but you don't want to fuckin' listen to me, do you?" Mitch said.

I saw this and started to turn around, but then Mitch wheeled on me and Meade. Now that we'd walked in, we were fair game.

"Sit the fuck down, the two of you. You're not going anywhere."

He was serious, I could tell. Hell, I wouldn't have wanted Mitch mad at me *without* a knife. With it, all he had to do was say jump, and I'd say, How high?

Somehow, Mitch got it in his head that Meade and I were being followed by the cops and they were outside, staking him out. So he told us to barricade the doors. We looked at him like he was crazy, which, at that moment, he was.

"You think I'm kidding? Do what I tell you," Mitch shouted.

Poor Meade; he was so scared, I swear he peed in his pants. I can't say I blamed him, either, because I was worried about how crazy Mitch might get. His temper was one thing; but that knife in his hand was another. I had no choice but to barricade the front door. We put a couch in front of it, then stacked two chairs on top of the couch. After that, Mitch ordered us to pull the blinds down on all the windows, then he ripped the phone out of the wall.

Finally, I tried to plead with him.

"Mitch, listen to me. It's okay, there's nobody out there," I said gently.

"You calling me a liar, motherfucker?" he shouted. He met my eyes with a gaze so fierce, I had to look away.

His girlfriend tried reasoning with Mitch, too.

"Kevin, stop acting so crazy, these people are your friends," she said. With that, Mitch turned to her and raised his anger to yet another level. Still holding the knife in his right hand, he grabbed his girlfriend's little cat, who had the misfortune to be walking near his feet at that very moment.

In one awful sweep of his hand, Mitch pulled the cat's head back, exposing its throat.

"You think I'm kidding when I say don't ever fuck with me?" he shouted. Before the girl could answer, Mitch took the knife to the cat, and cut its head off.

Clean.

I was horrified by the sight: Mitch was still holding the cat's head in one hand, while the body dropped to the floor, blood pouring out from where the head once was, limbs still twitching. The girl was practically out of control, screaming so loud I'm shocked the cops didn't actually show up. Meade tried to run for the door, but Mitch wasn't about to become reasonable yet.

"Sit the fuck down, Meade. You and Doc, sit down on that couch and don't move," he said.

Considering he had a severed cat's head and a knife in his hands, he didn't get an argument from either one of us.

We sat down. So did the girlfriend. And Mitch sat across from us, shooting darts at us with his eyes. Sort of like a modern-day Mexican standoff. We remained like this for almost two hours, no one saying a word, until Mitch finally started to nod off.

He'd start to close his eyes, then open them quickly, almost like he was testing us. Finally, for some reason, the dark cloud over him moved on. Mitch half smiled and said, "You guys can go."

We left, in about a half second, of course. The next day at the ballpark, I approached Mitch and asked, "You feeling okay?"

Looking straight ahead, he said, "Yesterday never happened." And we never mentioned it again.

OBVIOUSLY, MITCH WASN'T the only wild man in the clubhouse. And he wasn't the only one drinking. I'd say there were at least a dozen Mets who drank heavily after games in those years. And we had a growing drug problem, too, which had a foundation in the near-daily amphetamine use.

But drinking was where it all started for me. My journey would begin with beer, then it was on to gin or Rémy Martin. Eventually, alcohol became my bridge to drugs, but not yet. Not in 1985 or 1986. But my intoxication wasn't just physical. I was woozy with power, and more than anything else, that led to my downfall.

I mean, on Forty-second Street, there was a massive picture on the side of a skyscraper of me going into my windup, a paid advertisement from Nike. One of my favorite tricks in those days was to make sure I drove by that building whenever I was on a date. I wouldn't say a word, and just wait until the woman I was with noticed my image. It was guaranteed to impress.

Part of what made the Mets so good in the eighties was our recklessness. I don't just mean on the field, either. We had players who were unafraid of anything, anyone. Straw and Mitch were always looking to punch someone out, it seemed. There were so many days Darryl would say to me, "Doc, drill someone today, and if he charges the mound, me and Mitch will beat the fuck out of all of them."

For some reason, Strawberry hated the Reds' Tom Browning, and one day in '86 when Browning hit Tim Teufel with a fastball, Darryl and Mitch were the first out of the dugout throwing punches. Still, I don't think anyone on our team wanted to ever get into a boxing ring with our third baseman, Ray Knight, because we knew he was a former Golden Gloves champ and we saw what he did to the Reds' Eric Davis.

Davis, one of Darryl's closest friends growing up, slid hard into third base. He and Knight had words, and Eric made the mistake of shoving Knight. Ray responded with a quick, devastating right to Davis's jaw, precipitating a bench-clearing brawl. Back then, Dave Parker was the Reds' enforcer and he did plenty of talking after the game, telling reporters that if Knight was interested in fighting any more Reds, he'd be at the batting cage the next day.

Well, that's all Ray needed to hear. He wasn't afraid of anyone. In fact, the very next day when we were coming off the field from batting practice, Ray made a point of walking right toward Parker, who was leaning up against the batting cage. He knew that Parker had seen him, and we all watched to see what Dave would do.

Ray wasn't about to start a fight without provocation, but he made it known that he was there, in case Parker wanted to back up his words. The closer Knight got to Parker, the slower he walked, until he was taking baby steps around the cage. There was no mistaking his message. As it turned out, Parker wanted no part of him. He just kept leaning on the batting cage, staring out toward the outfield, pretending not to see Ray.

That incident set the tone for the rest of the '86 season. We had a ten-game lead by the middle of June, at which point Cardinals manager Whitey Herzog said, "No one's going to catch the Mets." He was right, of course. We stretched that margin to seventeen games by August, and we ended up winning the division by twenty-one and a half games.

We had talent, sure, but we also had incredible fire. Our spiritual leader was Keith Hernandez, the former Cardinal who was the co-winner of the National League's Most Valuable Player award in 1979. "Mex" was cool and tough and impossible to retire in late innings. There was something about Hernandez that made you play better, just being around him.

I mean, I could remember the way he'd stand on the top step of our dugout and intimidate opposing pitchers who'd gotten him out with curveballs or off-speed stuff.

"You're a fucking cunt, a pussy," Hernandez would shout. I'd be thinking to myself, What balls this guy has. No one talks like that in the big leagues anymore. The players are all friends, partly because of the bond the Players Association has forged. Back in the eighties, we still disliked our opponents.

Hell, Mex disliked even some of us. He seemed to strongly resent the influence that Gary Carter had on the pitching staff; that was one of Keith's strengths, his knowledge of opposing hitters and the way to best exploit their weaknesses.

There were many, many times Gary would come to the mound to discuss how we'd attack the next hitter—only to have Keith visit me the moment Gary started walking back to the plate.

"What did he say?" Hernandez asked, nodding toward Carter.

"He wants me to throw curveball," I'd said.

"Fuck that, throw your best fastball. Do what I tell you."

I would nod in agreement. Hell, I wasn't going to get into a fight with Mex. So Gary could never understand why, suddenly, I was shaking off the curveball that we'd just discussed throwing.

I remember in 1985, the New York *Post* ran a poll asking New Yorkers who was the best first baseman in the city, Keith or Don Mattingly. Somehow, Mattingly won by 12 percentage points, perhaps because he was in the middle of a monster season, when he ended up with a .324 average, including an American League–best 145 RBIs and thirty-five homers.

Keith batted .309 with ten homers and ninety-one RBIs, so in terms of pure numbers, Mattingly indeed was the superior player. But the fans couldn't have known how Hernandez single-handedly changed opponents' offensive strategies in late innings, because no one—not even Mattingly—could turn the 3–6 force-out on a bunt play better.

Mex had this uncanny ability to charge the bunt and come up throwing to second base all at once, as if he was a shortstop. Hernandez had a stronger arm than any first baseman around—again, stronger than Mattingly's—which meant other teams very rarely were able to put down a successful sacrifice bunt against us.

And there was no one in either league who kept up such a constant stream of chatter as Hernandez. Between him and Ray Knight, it was like having two in-game, on-the-field therapists. They kept me focused at all times on the mound.

Hernandez wasn't afraid to exercise his authority off the field, either, even with me. One night in June 1985, me and a couple of starting pitchers were playing Wiffle ball in the clubhouse during a game. That's wasn't entirely cool with Davey, but he also knew that as a pitcher who had nothing to do between starts, it's awfully difficult to spend every inning of every game on the bench.

I mean, there are days when baseball can numb the senses. So killing time in the clubhouse can be a way to preserve your sanity. Playing Wiffle ball with Sid Fernandez and Darling? Okay, maybe we shouldn't have been, but it bothered me that when Hernandez came in for a soft drink between innings, he singled me out, and no one else.

"Come on, Doc, there's a game going on out there," he said.

I didn't say a word. I waited until everyone returned to the dugout, making sure I was last. It offended me that we were all guilty of abusing Davey's trust in us, not just me.

To his credit, Keith apologized later in the game. Still, I decided to mess with him a little.

"Still my friend, Doc?" he asked.

Straight-faced, I said, "You've never been my friend, Mex."

We both laughed a moment later, but Davey got wind of the Wiffle ball incident and called a team meeting after the game, a 3–2 loss to the Cardinals.

"Maybe I should crack down," he said loudly, deciding everyone had to be on the bench at all times, except for the starting players, who were only allowed into the clubhouse for a drink or something. But as for the rest of us, no more sleeping in the trainer's room, no more cardplaying, no more watching TV in the players' lounge, and definitely, no more Wiffle ball games.

Part of our overall problem was that we could be hyper and combative.

What made us that way? Beyond our physical skills, a lot of us were so wired on amphetamines, half the time we weren't even aware of the way we behaved. Amphetamines were like a cure-all for a ballplayer who'd stayed out all night; they compensated for a lack of sleep or a hangover. They made you feel quick and alive, made every fastball look like a grapefruit. There were ten to twelve Mets who used beanies—or beans, as they were called—and at least three that I'd say were seriously addicted to them. By that, I mean they wouldn't even wait until game time to load up. They'd start in the middle of the afternoon, reload with two to three cups of coffee right before the first inning, and then drink at night to bring themselves back down.

I was so intrigued by the supposed wonders of beanies, I tried them, too. In fact, I pitched against the Braves one day in 1986, thinking that I could throw even harder than I was already throwing. What I didn't realize, however, was that amphetamines make a pitcher too jittery to focus. In other words, I was so out of control that when a ground ball was hit back to me, I saw three of them. Luckily I grabbed the one in the middle and made the play, but when I got back to the dugout the trainer, Steve Garland, knew immediately that I was speeding.

"Go inside to the clubhouse and drink some milk," he said. "That'll bring you back."

I felt bad for Garland, in a way. He was a sweet, sweet man, hardworking and funny, and everyone on the team liked him. For that reason, Met management eventually blamed Steve for our drug-and-alcohol problems, saying that a trainer surely had to know what was going on.

To that I say: Garland wasn't a cop, and by passing the buck to him, all it did was convince me the Mets knew there was an epidemic in the clubhouse and chose not to intervene. By 1986, the Mets had hired Dr. Alan Lans as a drug counselor/therapist on a consulting basis. So, obviously, the front office had to know there was something wrong. But no wanted to say anything because we were winning and we were drawing fans to the ballpark.

I can only say that alcohol is the main reason why my performance fell off in 1986. The atmosphere in the clubhouse was conducive to it; Darryl drank, so did Keith Hernandez, Lenny Dykstra, Wally Backman, Bobby Ojeda, even Davey Johnson, our manager, kept vodka in the refrigerator in his office. Davey clearly didn't have a drinking problem, and I take responsibility for my own actions.

I used to drink a little in high school, but I discovered in the minor league that beer is baseball's social glue.

It's what makes it possible for a black kid from Florida to get along with a street kid from Brooklyn, or a Midwestern farm boy. Or a very unique Californian named Lenny Dykstra.

Lenny and I played together in the minor leagues in Class A Lynchburg in 1983, and I could tell right away he had big plans for his future. "I'm going to The Show, dude," is what he'd tell everyone. The Show, of course, was what minor leaguers called the Major Leagues. And "dude" is what Lenny called everyone. It was his term of respect.

I found of Lenny had his own, brilliant way of using the English language—devised partly out of Southern California slang, MTV vernacular, and his own imagination.

In Lenny's world, when a man loved a woman, he would "weep" her. "Sweet" meant good, and "nails" meant very good. That's where Dykstra got his nickname, Nails, although most people thought he was referred to that way because he was so tough.

He was, of course. Lenny was all muscle, and played with a certain recklessness. Actually, I always thought he was a football player trapped in a baseball player's body and profession. With a bigger frame, he could've easily been an NFL linebacker; Lenny sure had the right mentality.

In 1983, Lenny batted .358 and stole 105 bases at Lynchburg, and he walked around with a confidence that was uncanny for someone who was only at Class A. Still, it's that ego that helped Lenny rise so fast in the organization—not just his skill.

It's amazing how many great ballplayers just shrivel up and die in the minors because they doubt themselves on the way up. The closer they get to the big leagues, the more intimidated they become, until they lose that edge that's so necessary.

Lenny never once suffered a confidence crisis. He never thought he wasn't good enough. He always told me, "I'm on my way, dude." And his positive nature paid huge dividends. When Dykstra finally made it to the big leagues in 1985, he instantly became one of our spark plugs—annoying pitchers, driving opposing catchers crazy by stealing bases, and playing a terrific center field.

I liked Lenny so much, I let him live in my house in '85, right after he was called up from the minors and needed a place to stay. I respected his drive, and I liked the way he could make me laugh. He was fun to listen to on the plane, and after a couple of drinks, we appreciated him even more.

One time, Lenny stood up and started teasing Tim Teufel, who was nursing a hamstring injury. Lenny started opening and closing his fist, as if milking a cow, making loud kissing sounds and telling Teufel, "Yeah, baby . . . milk that leg. Milk it good."

When I got to the big leagues, I found that drinking kept us from getting bored on long plane rides. It was almost like a caste system on those airplanes. The manager and the coaches sat up in first class, the rookies sat in the middle, and the veterans sat in the back and verbally abused everyone, especially when we got drunk.

It could get pretty vicious, depending on how long we'd been in the air, or how much we'd had to drink. That's when Darryl would be his meanest. He got on Gary Carter because he never went out at night. He got on Davey for using Lenny Dykstra more often than Mookie Wilson. Maybe the worst was how he used to taunt Tim Teufel, twisting around his nickname—which was Richard—into Richard Head. We all laughed about it, and for the most part, Darryl was just testing Teufel to see how much he could handle. Still, calling a teammate a dickhead was pushing it.

One day, Tuff decided he'd heard enough. Sitting five or six rows in front of Darryl, Teufel got up, turned around, and said, "I'm not going to take your shit anymore. That's the last time I'm listening to that."

I was stunned at how genuine Teufel's anger was; I guess he no longer cared how much bigger and stronger Darryl was, and, when provoked, how much more volatile he could be. But there comes a point where every man is ready to snap, and Teufel had obviously reached his.

Would he really have fought Darryl? No one found out, because a couple of us got in between the two; no punches were ever thrown. The irony is that Darryl never made fun of Teufel after that day. In fact, the two became great friends. Word got around the league that Teufel had stood up to Straw, and I swear, opposing players started to look at Tim in a different way. I think he was even pitched a little more cautiously.

The lesson, of course, is that as close as the Mets were in those days, we had our share of quarrels.

But Darryl and I were as close as brothers. And sometimes we fought, too. There was a brief skirmish on the charter flight from New York to Boston during the World Series. It was a little thing, but Straw was in one of his fighting moods. I asked the flight attendant for a drink, and I suppose she was busy, because she never came back.

A few minutes later I asked again, a little more impatiently, and Darryl went off on me.

"Doc, you think she's your servant or something?"

I couldn't believe how aggressive he was. With me, of all people.

"Hey, man, all I want is a beer," I said.

"Then wait your turn, man. She's busy, can't you see that?"

"Why don't you mind your own business, cuz. I ain't talking to you."

At that point Straw got up and said, "It is my business," and we were both ready to go. Once again, our teammates separated us, but it was obvious tensions were running high during the Series, especially since we'd lost Games One and Two at Shea and just about everyone thought we were finished.

The New York *Post* ran a huge back-page headline that read MEET THE MUTTS.

Nice. The National League champions, who'd won 108 regular-season games, were being called dogs by their hometown newspaper. There was enormous pressure on all of us because we knew we were so damn lucky to have beaten the Astros in the deciding Game Six of the League Championship Series.

By now, it's well-documented history that Mike Scott would've pitched against us had there been a Game Seven, and I have my doubts if we could've beaten him.

That might've explained why we tore up the plane that took us home from Houston. We'd just played 16 innings, a 7–6 victory that will go down as one of the most compelling October moments in baseball history.

Even though I didn't win either one of my starts against the Astros, I pitched well. I lost, 1–0, to Nolan Ryan in Game One, and had a no-decision in a 2–1 loss in Game Five. I allowed just one run in that game, too, which made me feel like I had a right to celebrate on that plane with everyone else.

To say we caused damage is a pristine way of putting it. It was a scene out of *Animal House:* food fights, heavy drinking, loud music, openly groping our wives and girlfriends, who were allowed on this one trip. At one point the partying was so out of control, the lavatory door accidentally flew open and there was one of my teammates, his face in front of lines of cocaine.

I wasn't shocked that he was using; I was shocked that he was so high, he didn't even realize the door was open. Still, I turned away and pretended not to see, but everyone did.

As for the rest of the Mets, they continued treating the plane like it was a fraternity house with wings, which is why, days later, the front office received a bill from TWA for $20,000. Frank Cashen, our general manager, handed the airline's letter to Davey Johnson, obviously expecting that we, the players, would come up with the cash.

Davey's response? In front of all us, he tore up the piece of paper and said, "Fuck 'em, if it wasn't for us, there wouldn't have been a reason to celebrate. Let Frank pay for it."

That's why we loved Davey so much; he was a renegade, just like us, and in the years when we enjoyed a talent gap over the rest of the National League, he was the perfect manager. But as the years passed, and some of us, like Hernandez and Carter, got older, Davey's magic stopped working. Suddenly his antiauthoritarian ways became an irritation to the front office.

Actually, Davey was always a pebble in Cashen's shoe, but by 1990, the GM was in a position to do something about it. When Davey got fired early in '90, I went home and cried. And I remember Darryl saying, "I'll never come back here." He was right, too. He signed with the Dodgers as a free agent, a parting that was precipitated, in part, because Davey was gone.

Thing is, Davey has won everywhere he's managed: the man just knew how to maximize the talent in his clubhouse, whether it was the Mets, or the Reds, or the Orioles. Ask him, though, and I bet he'll say no team gave him greater emotional satisfaction than the '86 Mets, because we were so damn good, and so damn lucky.

I mean, first we slithered by the Astros without having to see Mike Scott one last time. Actually, we knew that Scott was scuffing the ball, but the umpires were letting him get away with it. And that made him impossible to hit. Without a Game Seven against Houston, we felt bulletproof against the Red Sox. But that was before we were down 2–0 in the Series before we'd even blinked.

We lost Game One, 1–0, when Teufel let Rich Gedman's ground ball go through his legs in the seventh inning, scoring Jim Rice. Ron Darling pitched a great game, allowing only three hits and that one unearned run. But we couldn't touch Bruce Hurst. Darryl did lead off the ninth with a walk, but Calvin Schiraldi came in to get the last three outs.

One thing I'll always remember about Teufel that night: he stood in front of wave after wave of reporters, admitting that he simply messed up Gedman's grounder. That took guts, to tell a nation you made a mistake. Teufel was a man about it, and I respected his honesty.

In Game Two, the Sox's momentum kept growing, and much of that was my fault. I allowed home runs to Dave Henderson and Dwight Evans, and in all I surrendered five earned runs in five innings. We lost, 9–3, and it appeared our miracle machine had run out of horsepower.

But that was before we tied the Series, taking the next two games at Fenway, giving me a chance to put us ahead in Game Five on October 23. And once again, I came up short. In truth, I had nothing that night, allowing nine hits and four runs in just four innings. Hurst was again untouchable, and we went down, 4–2, as I took my second Series loss.

What followed, of course, is well-documented history. We broke the Red Sox's hearts in Game Six, when Mookie's ground ball whispered between Bill Buckner's legs. It was the most amazing display of fortune that I'd ever witnessed in baseball. We were down 2–0, with Roger Clemens shutting us out through the fifth, although we eventually tied the score at 3–3.

But Boston went ahead, 5–3 in the tenth inning against Rick Aguilera, on Henderson's solo HR and an RBI single by Marty Barrett. In the bottom of the tenth, after Hernandez and Wally Backman were retired, it looked like our season was over.

Hernandez, in fact, was already in Davey's office having a beer, watching what he thought was the final out. The dugout was in a state of shock; no one believed that we were actually about to go down. But then, history: Carter, Kevin Mitchell, and Ray Knight all singled off Schiraldi and when reliever Bob Stanley threw a wild pitch that scored Mitchell with the tying run, you could see the panic on the Red Sox's faces. Actually, it was closer to fear.

There was a noise that was coming from the stands that went beyond the definition of "loud." And I'm not even sure it could be called human. But the decibel level was so great at Shea, I believe the Red Sox were wilting because of it.

Mookie hit that legendary ground toward first base, and the question for the ages was: Even if Billy Buckner had caught it, would he have beaten Mookie to the bag? I doubt it. I think we would've beaten the Sox even without The Error, although we'll never know, because the last image I remember of Game Six was the ball whispering through Buckner's legs and the look of horror on Buckner's face when he realized that we'd just scored three runs with two out.

We were delirious at home plate, piling on top of each other like kids. I look at old videos from that game, and seeing our celebration still gives me chills. People ask me, what was my favorite, all-time Met memory, and it's exactly that: seeing Ray Knight landing on home plate and the riot that followed.

After that stunning finish, we just knew that we'd win Game Seven, too. Our karma was too perfect for the Series to end any other way. Even though Boston took a 3–0 lead on Darling in the second inning, we knew we'd eventually see Calvin Schiraldi again, and unlike Game One, we were determined to get to him. We knew the pressure would be more than Schiraldi—or any of the Red Sox—would be able to digest.

We scored three runs off Schiraldi in the seventh inning, part of a comeback that was sealed when Darryl hit a solo home run off Al Nipper, and Jesse Orosco hit an RBI single past a drawn-in Boston infield.

Ah, that last out will last a lifetime in my memory bank: Jesse striking out Marty Barrett, flinging his glove into the air and dropping to his knees, his fists raised to the sky. It was the greatest moment of my career, and the best team—on and off the field—that I ever knew. I only wish the Mets front office would recognize us, the '86 Mets, for the love affair we had with New York.

To this day, we haven't been formally invited back to Shea—

not for an Old-Timers' Day, or even just to throw out a first pitch. The Yankees have a viselike grip on New York, and the Mets have done nothing in response. The most beloved team in franchise history remains invisible to management, for reasons I can't understand. In fact, the Mets recently gave away my old number 16 to Hideo Nomo, which is further proof that the organization doesn't really appreciate us, or me.

I realize, of course, that I made bad decisions in those years, as we all did. But the Mets have forgiven other players—just this past year, in 1998, they signed Tony Phillips, who had been arrested in 1997 on a drug charge. If they could give Phillips a second chance, why not me and my teammates?

That World Series triumph should be like a shrine to the front office, and I say that even though I didn't do very well against Boston. All I can say is that I used up the last of my best fastballs in the League Championship Series against the Astros. In truth, I was running on empty.

That's part of the reason I partied so hard after Game Seven—I was happy for the team, glad to be part of something so wonderful. But I also wanted to forget how I almost cost us a chance to be world champs. I was drop-dead drunk that night—a nonstop alcohol binge that lasted until eight in the morning. And that's when I missed the parade in lower Manhattan.

Much has been made of my absence that day. There's certainly no excusing it—and no excuse. It was New York's way of expressing its thanks and admiration for the Mets, and I was too irresponsible to show up. There isn't a day that goes by when I don't think about it, and still regret it. But contrary to what so many rumors insist, I wasn't high that night, and the reason I slept through the festivities had nothing to do with drugs.

It was a simple, garden-variety hangover. I was home in Long Island, having partied heavily into the night at several clubs and after-hours clubs. I finally put my head on the pillow at eight, foolishly thinking a few minutes of napping would refresh me. Instead, the next sound I heard was a knocking on my front door.

It was Darryl, who'd told me the night before that he was coming to pick me up. I agreed to drive into Manhattan with him. I'd had every intention of going. In fact, I told Jay Horwitz to save a spot for me in one of the lead cars; I was that excited about it. But now that I was feeling like death, there was no way I was leaving the house.

Not for Darryl, not for the Mets. For no one.

I know Straw was deeply concerned, because he kept knocking and knocking on the door. Soon the knocking turned into pounding and I could hear the panic in his voice.

"Doc, you coming? Come on, we got to get to the parade," he said.

I'd pulled the curtain near by bed aside and watched him. I was touched by his consideration, and it took me many years to finally tell Straw that I'd seen him through the window. God, why couldn't I have just gotten out of bed, splashed some water on my face, put on a pair of sunglasses, and suffered through the headache and bad breath like everyone else on the team?

The reason, of course, was this lie that I lived: I didn't want people to see me in that condition. I didn't want anyone—fans, club officials, or the politicians—to know the humble, meek Doc was a drinker and could show up in public looking so bad. I had this image that I was required to maintain. At least that's what I thought. So I took the easy way out: I disappeared, I hid. I hoped the whole thing would just go away on its own.

It didn't. Of course it didn't. All my absence did was fuel speculation that I was a drug user, a whisper that'd been following me throughout the summer. People had been wondering about me all year, because I didn't dominate National League hitters the way I had in 1985. It was the drinking—excessive drinking that was a stepping-stone to eventual drug use.

The reason so many people suspected I was getting high in '86 was because I spent so much time with Darryl on the road, getting loaded deep into the night. And by then, even though I was unaware of it at the time, he was already using coke. Straw never admitted to that until many years later, which I guess I could understand. But he didn't think twice about implicating me when the front office heard rumors that a black Met superstar was involved.

That summer, Donald Fehr of the Players Association came to me and asked me if I'd agree to be tested. He said it'd be a good way to quell the rumors. I flatly said no, because I resented the implication that just because I wasn't as dominant as I was in 1985, it had to be because of drugs. A white player is allowed to fall off; if a black player suffers the same, one-year decline, then suddenly it's his "lifestyle" that's called into question.

Still, the whispers persisted that a black Met was heavily involved with cocaine. It was Ray Knight, no doubt speaking on behalf of management, who approached Darryl and asked who that player was. Strawberry told Knight, "It's Doc." He should've never said that, but as I came to learn soon after, Darryl was already using in '86 and was trying to cover his tracks.

For years, in fact, Darryl went out of his way to deflect attention from his drug use. In 1987, when I tested positive for cocaine, reporters naturally went to him and asked, "Should we fear for you, too?"

Straw said he wasn't raised that way, that he'd never considered using drugs. Eventually, Darryl was more open about his problems. Likewise, he corrected an assertion in his book, published in 1992, that I pitched under the influence of drugs in the '86 play-offs.

Straw later explained that those were the words of his ghostwriter, and that if he was guilty of anything, it was being too lax about the book's editorial content. I had to accept his word on that, because he knew better. I did not use drugs in 1986, neither in the regular season nor in the play-offs nor World Series.

But that didn't mean I wasn't headed for trouble. In fact, I was walking a straight line toward disaster soon after I returned home to Tampa in late October 1986.

## MAY 14, 1996 (CONTINUED)

I PULLED INTO the players' parking entrance at the Stadium, which is right across the street from the ballpark itself. I'd only been with the Yankees for two months, but I'd already sensed how much energy they were generating. It was only three P.M., and already there were fans waiting at the gates, hundreds of them, looking for autographs, or even just a hello from the players.

I believed that was one reason the Yankees had such a hold on the city in the mid-nineties, for the simple reason that fans were able to see the players arrive at the park, in street clothes. Even if it was just for a moment, it allowed the public to see us as we really are—that Paul O'Neill drives a Ford Explorer or that David Wells wears baggy shirts.

Me, I usually tried to sign a few autographs or chat with some of the kids at the door—at least on the days I wasn't pitching. But when I was starting, I had a strict rule for myself, which was: no interviews, no autographs, nothing that would take me too far away from the game I was about to pitch.

Some guys are so casual about their pregame routine, it amazes me. I mean, Coney would be doing interviews with the press an hour before he was supposed to take the mound, which is when my adrenaline is starting to surge. I didn't know how David could be that easygoing, but I needed time to think of how I was going to pitch great hitters like Griffey.

No question, this was the worst possible day to face the Mariners, the defending Western Division champions. I was exhausted, totally unfocused on the game, and worried about my father's heart transplant that was going to take place the next morning.

Stories about my dad's illness had been in the papers the few days before this, and it seemed everyone in the ballpark had a sense something was wrong. The cops, who were normally very friendly to me, just nodded politely. Same thing with the security guards, even the clubhouse kids. Walking into the clubhouse itself, I felt a strange wall around me.

I sat at my locker a moment, wondering who I should talk to, with whom I could share this burden. Coney was my best friend on the team, but he wasn't around. And if it'd been another era in my life, I could've reached out to Darryl Strawberry, the closest friend I ever had in baseball. But he was still in the independent Northern League, trying to work his way back to the big leagues after a tax problem and drug suspension.

Actually, the person who could've helped me most was my pitching coach, Mel Stottlemyre, who'd been with me ever since my rookie year in 1984. Mel was almost like a second father to me—patient, yet disciplined. Kind, but tough enough to get in my face when necessary. We'd been through a lot, me and Mel, in the last twelve years, and I think he knew this emergency was destroying me on the inside.

"Doc, you got a second?"

I looked up and realized it was, in fact, Mel who'd come by my locker. He had this gentle smile on his face, but there was no disguising the concern behind it.

"Joe wants to see you in his office."

We walked in together, with Mel shutting the door behind us. Joe was sitting behind his desk, looking at the unlit cigar on his desk as if he'd been about to fire it up. But not now. Like Mel, the concern on Joe's face was obvious.

I hadn't really known much about Joe Torre in the years I was with the Mets, only that he managed the Cardinals through some decent seasons, and for the most part, his players liked him. Actually, the rap on Torre was that he was too easygoing, which I never understood once I'd learned a little about his ways.

Torre was a little like Davey Johnson, in that he trusted his players to think and act like adults. Davey might've been a little more of a renegade, but both were good managers who had the respect of everyone in the clubhouse. Both of them were enormously successful Major Leaguers in their time, and if that offered any advantage, it's that they understood what it meant to stand in a player's shoes.

Joe, especially, used to tell people that as a former National League batting champion in 1971, he knew how easily a player could hit .371 one year, and then not even break .300 the following year. So much of being on top of your game starts in your head, and if there was problem outside the ballpark—like in a hospital in Tampa—there was no reason to fight it.

"Listen, I want to tell you this one more time, just so you're clear on the decision you make tonight," Torre said to me. "You don't have to pitch this game. We have plenty of arms. If you feel your father needs you there, if you have to be with your family, you leave right now. Take as long as you need. And I don't want to come back up here until you feel everything's okay."

Joe's generosity was enormous—so much so that I almost was rendered speechless by it. In a way, I'd almost hoped he'd make the decision for me. Either order me to get on that plane, or else put the baseball in my hand and tell me to strike out fifteen, to do it for my dad.

Oh, I tried that little trick in my head, already. I told myself, I'll stay up here and dedicate the game to him. That would give me the inspiration—or was it the rationalization?—I needed to pitch. That might've worked in Little League, but these were the

Mariners. What if I got my ass kicked? How would I explain that?

The Mariners were sure capable of beating up a pitcher who didn't have his best stuff. Hell, they were confident enough to light up even the best pitchers in the game, even on the nights they had their A-game.

I paid close attention to the Mariners-Yankees showdown in the 1995 division series. I was almost living those games, pitch by pitch, in my house in St. Petersburg, because that was the time George Steinbrenner and I were talking about a contract. I wasn't rooting against the Yankees, but I knew George's need for another starting pitcher would intensify if the Yankees lost.

It wasn't until the next spring that I heard how bad it'd been in the clubhouse after that last loss in Seattle. Some guys were crying, including Don Mattingly, and it was the end for Buck Showalter and the general manager, Gene Michael.

In a sense, that defeat in Game Five made it possible for me to return to New York, the place I'd left so darkly in 1994. And the more accustomed I became to being a Yankee, the more I appreciated what they'd done for me—signing me when I was in the ash heap, fighting back from a cocaine addiction. Where were the Mets when I really needed them?

I owed the Yankees, now and for the rest of my career. Maybe that's why I made one more phone call before I decided which path to take. I reached for the phone on Torre's desk, and asked simply, "Is it okay?"

Joe nodded. "Absolutely." Then he started to get up, both he and Mel, as if to leave the room.

"No, it's okay," I said. "It's only going to be a minute."

I dialed St. Joe's and spoke to the nurse on duty. By now, she recognized my voice and knew exactly why I was calling. There was no change, she said. He's hanging in there. We're all praying for him.

That's all I wanted to hear. As long as they said there'd been no downturn, I was going out to the mound. I put the phone down and looked at Torre and Mel, both of whom had moved respectfully a few feet away, to give me as much privacy as possible in those few moments.

"Any news, Doc?" Torre asked.

"Same," I said.

I took a deep breath, and said, finally, "If it's okay with you, I'm staying and I'm going to pitch. I don't know what I have—I might end up embarrassing myself out there—but I'm going to walk out there. I'm doing it for my dad."

For a moment Joe just looked at me, wanting to say something that I knew was coming from his heart. But I don't think he could find the words. Instead, he gave me this half smile and said, "You're going to be fine."

# THREE

IT WAS ABOUT a week after the World Series, when I'd been to my fourth party in a row, that I finally opened the front door to hell. I didn't realize it at the time, because I still thought of myself as physically invincible, but I was about to learn otherwise.

I was in a side room in a large house. There were hundreds of people inside, it seemed, all of them glad-handing me, telling me what a great Series I had. That should've been a tip-off. I'd had an embarrassingly bad Series, but they didn't care. To them, I was a celebrity and all they wanted to do was suck up to me.

The funny thing was, I couldn't really understand their admiration. When I looked in the mirror, I was just an ordinary guy who preferred to look up to a third cousin—the guy who owned the house, the one who threw the party.

He was much older than me. He was always the biggest and baddest guy on the block; nobody fucked with him.

He was also a drug dealer.

Somehow, my cousin's failing didn't seem so bad. I mean, I'd seen junkies strung out on the street, and he wasn't anything like that. He drove a nice car, had a great sense of humor, seemed to be far cooler than anyone I'd ever known. Nothing pleased me more than when he bragged to his friends about me.

"Doc Gooden, that's my blood," he'd say.

All I wanted was his approval—which was pathetic, I know. Here I was, a grown man, an accomplished professional athlete, very possibly on my way to the Hall of Fame, and I was worrying about being liked by a guy who saw reality through the prism of a cocaine high.

I guess it was inevitable that, sooner or later, my cousin would offer me the drug. I guess he saw it as a badge of honor, that Doc Gooden—Mr. Met—had gotten high with him. I'd seen my share of drugs around the Mets, and of course, growing up in Tampa. I was foolish enough to try to buy some back when I was a senior in high school, just because someone dared me and I thought it'd be cool to say I did.

I approached a dealer that everyone knew, named Hawk. He was a nice guy, and I could tell he liked me. In fact, he was always telling me that he enjoyed watching me pitch for Hillsborough HS. How he saw me, I'll never know, because Hawk was never in the stands. Maybe he watched from his car—a fine, shiny, black Mercedes.

Either way, Hawk was following my career and used to tell me I'd end up in the big leagues. As I came to find out later in life, Hawk used to brag to other drug dealers that he was friends with the rising star Doc Gooden, and it wasn't even a drug bond. He was proud of the fact that he *didn't* sell to me.

But I guess I was curious about coke. Curious and nervous. I approached him one day after practice. Even before I walked up to him, near a public playground, I was starting to sweat.

"Doc, everything cool?" he said in that easy way of his.

I said yeah, I was fine . . . and then I blurted it out.

"Listen, Hawk, I think I wanna buy. You got some?"

I still remember the way his eyebrows turned into little arches.

"You?"

"Yeah."

There was a silence for a moment, and I could see that Hawk was thinking.

"I'll hook you up," he said finally, "but not right here."

We walked to his Mercedes, got in, and we started to drive.

"You gettin' nervous, my little brother?" Hawk asked with a smile. I said no, even though I was scared out of my mind. What was I doing? All I wanted was to buy some coke, not actually get high. That way I could at least tell my friends I'd made a score with the famous Hawk and people would think I was using, which would've made me seem cool enough.

But I was getting in deeper than I'd planned. We were driving farther and farther away from my neighborhood, and at one point, at a stop sign, I almost bolted from the car. But the fear of people finding out I ran away from Hawk kept me frozen. I had lost control of the situation.

Finally, we pulled to a building in a part of town I was unfamiliar with. It was old and dirty and dangerous looking. Why couldn't Hawk have just sold me the coke right there at the playground? Instead, he pointed to the building in front of us and said, "Go to apartment Three C. My guys will take care of you. They're waiting for you."

"They?" I asked stupidly. "Who's they? How do they know I'm coming?"

"Just do what I tell you," Hawk said. I turned to him, and realized his smile was gone now. His face was like stone.

"Go."

As it turned out, I was about to get the lesson of my life. Hawk sent me into an apartment that was empty except for a table, a telephone, and two of the strongest, most terrifying dudes I'd ever seen. I literally couldn't keep my hands from shaking when I walked through that door, and my voice had risen an octave when I finally said I'd been sent by Hawk.

"Hawk says you got something for me," I stammered.

One of the guys just snickered. "Oh, yeah. We do."

That was the last thing I remember. The other guy, who was standing off to my right, punched me so hard in the face, my eyes rolled back into my head. He followed up with a blow to my ribs that must've knocked me completely off my feet, because for a second I felt like I was flying. Then I crashed onto the hardwood floor, desperately trying to breathe. I'd had the wind knocked out of me, and I was defenseless against these two bigger, stronger, and obviously angrier opponents.

I stayed down. There was no point in getting up, not unless I wanted to get killed. I actually thought I was going to die when I felt someone pull my head up so that it faced the ceiling. It was Hawk.

"Next time you wanna buy, little brother, I just might sell it to you," he said. "Now get the fuck out of here. And don't ever come back."

WITH THAT KIND of introduction to drugs, no wonder I stayed away. Until 1986, coke was about angry, violent people who would kill you if you looked at them the wrong way. But that all changed when my cousin offered me some.

Unlike Hawk, I could trust my cousin. He wouldn't hurt me. And like I said, I wanted to impress him. So when he razor-bladed four lines in front of me, I said yes.

I wish there'd been an alarm going off in my head, flashing DANGER, DANGER. I wish I'd let register the damage drugs had done to the careers and reputations of so many players I knew—including my own teammate Keith Hernandez, who'd been forced to testify in the Pittsburgh drug trials in 1985. Hell, I wish the cocaine I ingested didn't make me feel so damn good. But none of that happened. There was no last line of defense when I took my first hit.

Nobody scolded me, no one told me I was about to throw away some of my greatest accomplishments in baseball. And there sure wasn't any thunderbolt from the sky. It was just me, my smiling, smooth-talking cousin, and this drug, my personal demon.

I'd have been better off if I had a bad physical reaction to coke, which is the reason I hate Copenhagen, the snuff tobacco that so many players use today. I was curious in the minors leagues why so many of my teammates enjoyed chewing tobacco, but I couldn't stomach the idea of shoving a fistful of tobacco leaves in my mouth. So one of my buddies suggested Copenhagen in "dip" form—meaning, just a pinch between the gum and my lower front teeth.

The tobacco couldn't have been in my mouth for more than thirty seconds when I became nauseous and light-headed. It was awful, almost as if I'd been poisoned. I'm sure I would've vomited right there in the dugout had I not spit the Copenhagen out of my mouth and drunk about a gallon of cold water. The whole experience was over quickly, but the impression has lasted a lifetime. I can't even look at the small, circular tub of Copenhagen without remembering how sick I became, and that, more than anything, has kept me away from that ugly, cancer-related habit.

I wish I'd had the same reaction to the cocaine. But I didn't. A few hits of the drug, and I was on a happy, gentle journey. I was free from my insecurities, thrilled to have pleased my cousin, fully empowered to talk to everyone at the party, including the women.

The high came and went, lasting a few pleasant hours. I went home that night and although I was unaware of it at the time, I started down the road to addiction. It wasn't a headfirst dive into uncharted waters. I sort of tiptoed my way into this underworld. I waited about four or five days after that party to try it again; this time it was with a small group of buddies. Initially, I was using twice a week: then, subtly, without ever having made a conscious decision to increase, I was getting high three times a week.

At what point does a user officially become an addict? Maybe it's when he misses appointments, when he stays out all night and sleeps all day. When he experiences awful mood swings. When he finds himself daydreaming about getting high, and uses it as a reward for staying clean.

That's how the demon got inside of me—in a slow, insidious way, so cleverly that I was never aware of it. My mother sensed something was wrong. She asked constantly that winter, "Doc, are you using drugs?" I'd pretend to be outraged by the question, but there was no hiding my unusual behavior and the fact that I was dead asleep in the middle of the afternoon, seemingly every day.

My dad didn't catch on as quickly. He'd merely say I was getting my rest after a tough season.

"If he didn't have a job, that'd be another thing," Dad would tell Mom. "But this is his vacation, so leave him alone."

Soon, though, not even my dad would be able to rationalize my long disappearances. I'd be asked to run to the grocery store for some bread, and then not come back for two days. Vacation? It was more like self-destruction.

Since I was keeping late hours and running around with a crowd that didn't mind trouble, it wasn't long before I raised the antennae of the Tampa police. It was a bad winter for relations between the black community and white police officers, as I soon came to learn. Just after I returned home from the World Series, a sixteen-year-old black kid was shot fleeing from the cops after they said he'd fired a .38 into a group of bystanders. No gun was ever found.

Two months later another black man was killed by a cop who applied a choke hold to his carotid artery after he supposedly brandished a knife. Although the 911 call from neighbors said the man was threatening to kill his wife with the knife, after the struggle, cops realized there was no weapon. In April 1987, two cops struggled fiercely with a black drifter who was collecting bottles in a junkyard. The man died of a heart attack during the fight.

It was against this backdrop that I had my own war with the Tampa police. Many nights that winter, for no apparent reason, I'd been followed in my car on the way home. I could count at least 10 incidents of seeing a police car right in the rearview mirror, sometimes for miles and miles, only to have an officer pull me over and ask for my license and registration.

There'd never be an explanation, just a sneering cop who enjoyed giving me a hard time. I know they have a job to do, and no lawful society can exist without the presence of a professional police force. But there's a difference between protection and harassment, and there's no question that like many other young black men in the Tampa area, I was being bothered because of the color of my skin.

On December 13, 1986, my relationship with the Tampa police went from cold to violent. I was part of a caravan that was coming back from a basketball game at the University of South Florida. Traveling with me, in separate cars, were my nephew Gary, my friend Vance Lovelace, and three other acquaintances. I was driving my Mercedes 500SL with a friend named Troy in the passenger seat, Gary was in a Corvette, and one of the other guys was behind the wheel of a Nissan 280ZX.

We'd just pulled out of Chili's, where we'd had a bite to eat, and the cop saw a group of black guys in fancy cars and decided to pull us over. Obviously, he was on a fishing trip, looking for trouble. The first guy the cop targeted was Gary, engaging the police car's dome lights as soon as we all pulled away from a red light. But I'm sure Gary never saw the lights in his rearview mirror, because the stereo speakers in his car took up most of the space in his rear window.

The cop had a choice: either he pursued Gary, pulling up alongside him, or else he could simply go for the next target, which happened to be me. He chose me. I pulled over, and already in a bad mood, already sick of being baited by the cops, I prepared for the worst.

"Let me see your license and registration," the cop said, his voice full of belligerence.

"What's the reason that you pulled me over?" I asked, just as pointedly. Immediately I could sense there was a crisis building, and yet I was powerless to stop it.

"Don't worry about it, just get out of the car."

"Get out of the car? What did I do? Why are you guys always harassing me?"

"Who's harassing you? You've got a big fucking mouth," he said cruelly.

And here is where I crossed the line. I got in the cop's face and shouted, "No, *you* have a big fucking mouth."

"Oh, yeah? Now you're going to jail," he said.

His face had become a mixture of triumph, because he'd successfully baited me, and rage, because I had just cursed him. The cop reached for his handcuffs, and I panicked, thinking he was going for his gun. I don't know why I reacted this way, but I put my hands on the cop's, to stop him, and just at that moment at least fifteen squad cars pulled up. That was my bad luck.

The arriving cops thought I was trying to steal their partner's gun, which, I guess, explains why they were so aggressive with me. In their minds, they were saving another cop's life. I heard shouting and car doors slamming and the sound of heavy shoes pounding against the pavement. And then, a flurry of punches and kicks and choke holds unlike anything I'd ever experienced. Instantly, I'd been knocked to the ground, overpowered by I don't know how many officers. It felt like a hundred. What I was sure of was that this was more than an arrest; it was a lesson I was being administered. I was handcuffed and my feet were shackled. Once I was no longer able to defend myself, I was hit on the back, shoulders, arms, and legs with more fists and nightsticks. A female officer took the cheapest shot of all, slamming me across the face with her flashlight.

"Break his arm. Break his fucking arm," I heard one cop shout. Obviously, they knew who I was. In fact, I think the first officer was aware of my identity before he ever got out of his car. By now, my friends in the other cars had pulled over, mortified by what they were seeing. Gary tried to come to my rescue, but he was knocked to the ground, savagely punched and kicked, too.

Incredibly, Troy escaped undetected and unharmed. As soon as the first cop got me out of the car, Troy opened up the passenger-side door and ran away. And no one ever saw him fleeing. It was just as well, because no one could've helped me.

In fact, a white bystander who'd witnessed everything rushed up to one of the cops and pleaded for my safety.

"Leave him alone! What did he do?" the bystander asked. "Why are you doing this?"

A cop shouted back, "Get the fuck out of my face or else you're going to get arrested, too."

Meanwhile I was being beaten so relentlessly, and the choke hold that was being applied to my neck was so tight, the only way to live through it was to pretend I was dead. I closed my eyes and went limp, until I heard one of the cops say, "He's out, he's out!"

I let them carry me into the backseat of a squad car, still pretending to be unconscious. The cops then drove me to a dog track about two miles away. The place was dark, utterly empty, and now, for the first time, it occurred to me that I was going to be murdered.

Then I felt my eyelids being peeled back and a flashlight being shone into them. A pair of paramedics had arrived, which meant I wasn't going to die. I was hoisted into an ambulance and I realized I was being escorted by two new cops—two black cops.

This was the police department's way of handling the racial aspects of this incident. How could anyone complain about a black man who'd nearly been beaten to death if the arresting officers were also black?

I had four hours to think about that, all alone in the county jail's holding cell. All night, cops kept walking by me, looking at me like I was some kind of murderer.

I knew I was wrong to mouth off to that officer, and trying to stop him from handcuffing me was dumb. Still, nothing I did or said merited such a vicious beating. One or two officers could've easily taken control of the situation—arrested me, if that's what they really thought was right. But the force they used was so excessive, it's a wonder my arm didn't break and that my skull didn't split in half.

Even hours later, when tempers had cooled, the cops wouldn't tell me what'd happened to Gary or Troy. It wasn't until my parents came to bail me out that I learned Gary had been taken to the sheriff's-office jail. Finally, we all met at the house, paranoid and nervous, convinced the cops were waiting for us to go back outside so they could kill us.

I will confess that I was no longer thinking straight. In fact, I was consumed by images of revenge. My cousin—yes, that one, my link to cocaine—came by the house and kept telling me, "You can't let them get away with this. They started a war, man, and now it's up to us to finish."

My cousin looked at me, his eyes burning fiercely, as he asked, "What're you gonna do about this, Doc?"

Without hesitating, I said, "Someone has to pay."

And so we hatched a plan: seven of us would pile into my

cousin's pickup truck that night, riding around Tampa, speeding, violating as many traffic laws as we could in the hope that we'd be pulled over by a cop.

The revenge we sought was indeed real: we were all carrying automatic weapons and were prepared to use them. Was I crazy to be thinking this way? Absolutely. But was I crazed by the treatment I'd received? No question. We went out at ten P.M. and for the next thirty minutes, I was part of a posse that was ready to shoot the first unlucky officer we saw.

We tried desperately to get someone's attention. We must've been traveling over eighty miles an hour on Dale Mabry Boulevard, the main drag. We punched every red light, weaved in and out of traffic with total disregard for the safety of the other motorists. We sat there in silence, clutching the guns in our hands, not thinking of the consequences or the unfairness of this insane plot.

After all, there was no guarantee—indeed, no probability—that the cop we'd find would've been one of those involved in the melee. Chances are we would've stumbled upon an innocent officer, maybe even a great guy, and he would've met with terrible violence. And I would've either spent the next twenty years in jail, or else been shot. At the very least, my baseball career would've been over.

For thirty minutes, as we continued to drive, I thought about that. I can only believe it was God who protected me and the officers, who, for some reason, never pulled us over.

It's not as if the police saw us and decided against taking action. We simply didn't find any cops. Not one. Finally, after an hour, my anger began to dilute, and when we began a second trip around Tampa, I said to my cousin, "That's it, man. Let me out. It's not worth it."

No one argued with me. No one tried to talk me out of it. It was, after all, my beef with the cops, not anyone else's. I got off on Dale Mabry and called my mother. I asked her to pick me up, and the next day my cousin told me the rest of the guys decided to go home, too.

In retrospect, it was a terrifying look into my own soul. I saw how much anger I had stored up, and to what lengths I would go to satisfy my rage. There isn't a day that goes by when I don't thank God for saving me from that dark moment.

# FOUR

IT WAS IN the winter of 1986–87 that I started getting serious with Monica Harris. Actually, I'd known her since my Little League days, since her brothers were my teammates. I didn't notice her much back then, since she's four years younger than me, but by 1985 I realized how good-looking she'd become.

I saw this because Monica worked at a Burger King that was near a skating rink where everyone would hang out. It wasn't tough for me to get a date around Tampa, because by '85 everyone knew me. So one day when I drove up to place an order, there Monica was, taking orders. I tried the smooth, popular, athlete-of-the-world approach that, so far, hadn't failed.

"Hey, how's your family? Everything good with your brothers?" I asked. "When are we going to hook up?"

Monica looked at me like I was crazy, because I had another girl in the car with me. I didn't care. I was that impressed with

Monica, although, not surprisingly, she more or less told me to get lost.

"I don't think we're going out anytime soon," she said, nodding at the other woman in the car with me.

"Just a friend," I said, not caring if the other woman heard me or not.

It took several months of trying to get her to say yes, but Monica and I finally started dating; we went to the movies, we went out to eat, we would spend hours and hours talking about everything and nothing. I suppose what impressed me most about her was her calm. In a way, Monica was a lot like my mother.

And I also liked that she had no real interest in baseball, which meant she wasn't interested in my growing celebrity. She liked me for who I was. And she sure didn't care about my money, either. She had her own job, her own car, and was self-sufficient. And believe it or not, I admired the way Monica made me wait before going out with me. She had the guts to say no, just to see if I would come back. It confirms an age-old axiom about men, the one that says a guy will never have a long-lasting respect for a woman who gives in too easily. And Monica definitely did not.

Yet, with the growing closeness I had with her that off-season, I still wasn't able to tell her about my involvement with drugs. That was a secret, because I hadn't really admitted it to myself, although Monica was intuitive enough to know something was very wrong with the way I was living.

For instance, she and I would be driving sometimes in separate cars to dinner, and I'd let myself get caught at a red light. As Monica drove away, I'd turn around as soon as the light was green and see one of my cocaine-using buddies to get high. Hours later I'd tell Monica that I'd had a flat tire.

At first she believed me, but then she started to suspect that I was lying. She never considered the possibility that I was using drugs, however; in fact, she was convinced that I was seeing another woman. I was so depraved I allowed Monica to think that, just to keep my drug use covert.

I even went as far as to lie to the Mets in spring training. I called Davey Johnson from home, saying my best friend had been in a car wreck and that I had to see him in the hospital. The truth was, I'd been high the night before and was in no condition to play baseball. In fact, I was still high when I made the phone call. So I made an excuse, which Davey graciously accepted. But I doubt I was fooling anyone.

I say this because the Mets came to me that spring and asked if I would agree to undergo periodic and random drug tests. Actually, it'd been a back-and-forth issue all winter between Al Harazin, who was one of the club's vice presidents, and my agent, Jim Neader.

On March 24, the two of them agreed to include a drug-testing clause in my contract, which called for one test in spring training and two more during the regular season. I had the option of postponing the test, but the Mets seemed very aggressive and determined about it. They were obviously concerned about the leftover rumors from the '86 season and maybe my behavior in spring training.

I know this much: on March 25, I got high with two other Mets. They know who they are. They snorted so much damn coke, they asked me to run over to Tampa to buy more from my cousin. I knew we had practice early the next morning in St. Petersburg, so I said no.

"I'm done for the night," I said.

I knew I'd angered them, because a coke user knows no greater enemy than the voice of temperance. Not that I was a model of good behavior—far from it. But in this one particular instance, my need for coke didn't match theirs.

I suspect my refusal to indulge their appetite led them to turn me in to the Mets.

I believe this because the next day—the very next day—trainer Steve Garland came to me and said it was time for my drug test. I was stunned: when I agreed to let the Mets test me, I thought it'd be in a week or so. Never did I think I'd be policed that quickly.

Of course, I did have the right to say no, but I chose not to because I had no idea that the cocaine in my system would show up on the test. That's how little I knew about these exams, and how clueless I was about the way the body metabolizes drugs. I figured that since I was an athlete and sweated a lot, it would just pass right through me. But it was more than an athlete's arrogance, to be honest. It's the credo of any drug user, who believes that somehow, his lies will be believed. That he'll never get caught.

So, given that assumption, as false as it was, I thought it'd look suspicious to agree to drug testing, then refuse the Mets' very first request. When Garland asked for that urine sample, I complied, and thought nothing of it for the next four days.

I was busy trying to get ready for the season, which was ten days away. We were the defending world champs, and I was anxious to make up for my forgettable performance in the World Series. I still had hopes of re-creating 1985.

So I was a little surprised when I pulled into the parking lot at the Mets' spring training complex and saw that Joe McIlvaine, who was also now a vice president, was waiting for me.

"Frank wants to see you in his office, Dwight," Joe Mac said. "You don't have to get dressed this morning."

That was odd: one of the rules that Davey was so firm about was being on the field promptly at 9:30 A.M., and if I had to detour to Cashen's office, how could I be on time? Then I saw that Jim Neader's car was in the parking lot, too, which led me to believe that he and Cashen had agreed to a contract extension. Now it made sense: the Mets wanted my signature on a new deal.

Yes. All the sense in the world.

That assumption evaporated the moment I walked into Cashen's office. There, I saw Neader with an expression on his face that can only be described as pure horror. Cashen looked equally crushed. In fact, the little GM never looked so old and small as he did in telling me the drug test had come back positive.

"Son, we have a problem here. You're going to have to make some choices right away," Cashen told me.

My first instinct was to deny, to lie. I told Cashen there was no possible way that test could be correct, that I didn't do drugs, I'd never done drugs, and that there must've been some mistake.

Frank just shook his head.

"There's been no mistake," he said. "Is there anyone you want to call?" It was only then that I realized my world was starting to collapse. I'd been caught, and nothing could save me. Neader was powerless, as were my bosses. I could see how much Frank was hurt by this; I could only imagine what the news would do to my parents.

How could I possibly tell them? What would I say? I had to spare them. Only, how? Cashen explained that I had two options: I could serve a season-long suspension without pay, or else enter a rehab program. Obviously, I couldn't withstand the financial hit that a year's suspension would bring. If nothing else, my parents needed me to support them. But rehab? Getting locked in a room with a bunch of junkies?

It all hit me so hard, I put my head on the table and started to cry. The room went quiet as Cashen half turned away from me, partly to give me whatever privacy the little office could afford, but also because he was obviously saddened and disgusted by my downfall.

He waited a few more moments out of respect, but then pushed forward.

"We're going to have to move on this," Cashen said. "You're going to have go home and get yourself ready."

The Mets wanted to send me to the Smithers Institute for Rehabilitation in Manhattan, a 28-day program that was supposed to be one of the best in the country. I had no choice but to say yes; actually, that was the easiest crossroads I faced. The hard part was telling my parents.

I left the complex in a daze, numb as I started up the engine of my Mercedes. Normally, the drive from the spring training site in northeast St. Pete to my home in Tampa took thirty-five to forty minutes in rush-hour traffic, but it felt like I was pulling up to the driveway in five minutes.

The whole time, I was trying to think of a way to soften the blow to my mom and dad. How does a child possibly tell his parents that he's made such a horrible mistake? I took a deep breath as I prepared to open the front door, asking God for His help one more time. Still, I knew I was on my own when I walked into the kitchen and saw the look of surprise on my mother's face.

"Dwight, what's wrong?" she asked. Funny how all mothers have a built-in crisis detector. She knew instantly I was in trouble.

"Mom, I have something I want to tell you and Dad," I said. The three of us sat on the couch in the living room, where I explained what'd just happened to me.

"I have some good news and some bad," I said. "The bad news is that I tested positive for cocaine. The good news is that I'm going to go away and get some help. I'm going to fight this thing."

Upon hearing this, my mom's hand flew up to her mouth, a gesture I'd never seen her make. She was horrified. But even worse was my father's reaction—which was pure silence. He just looked at me, his eyes cutting me to shreds. Not once all morning did

Dad speak. I knew I must've crushed him; it was so obvious he was incapable of digesting this awful event.

What I really wanted was my father to say something, anything. To tell me that I'd broken his heart. To shake me and ask, "How could you do this to your career? To your family? To yourself?" There's no answer that I could've given him, but to at least hear his voice would've given me an outlet for my own pent-up suffering.

I knew that within an hour or two the Mets would be forced to announce the results of my drug test, which meant the reporters would soon be flocking to the house. I was no stranger to the media, naturally, but my parents were unprepared for the waves of ravenous reporters who sensed a huge story breaking.

There was no avoiding it, so I tried to think of ways to kill time. I walked from room to room, tried to flip through magazines or else watch a little TV, even tried unsuccessfully to take a nap. Nothing worked. There was no place to hide from the awful silence that filled the house. It felt so strange to be home at ten in the morning, removed from baseball, with nothing to do. My mom reached for her own form of therapy, which was cooking. At least I still had an appetite. But we were low on groceries, prompting her to make a shopping list and head off to the supermarket.

I hadn't noticed the cluster of reporters and TV crews on our front lawn until my mom opened the front door. And then it was like an explosion of snapping lenses and barked questions and rolling tape. My mother was deluged and I felt enormously guilty for the shame I put her through.

Then I realized: it wasn't just today's episode that devastated my parents. This had been going on for months, during all those nights when I didn't come home, when I didn't bother to tell my parents where I was going or where I'd been. When I didn't care how much they'd worried. When I snapped at my mother for no good reason, when I chose to sleep off a hangover or a high instead of spending time with my dad.

That's when I realized: drugs weren't just killing me. They were killing everyone around me, especially my parents, the two people in the world who loved me the most.

How could I possibly ask for their forgiveness? What would it take to win back their trust? And, professionally, what path did I need to travel to convince the Mets and their fans that I wasn't a loser and a junkie?

Yes, I boarded a jet from Tampa to New York on April 3, and I was heading directly to Smithers. But I was determined to get in and out of the program as quickly as possible. I wanted to show the world that Doc was okay, that I'd had just a freak slipup, and would soon be back on the mound blowing that fastball by National League hitters again.

A junkie? An addict? Not me. Not ever.

I spent those twenty-eight days in the rehab program, the whole time thinking that I didn't belong there. That was an awful mistake on my part; it was an athlete's arrogance and an addict's denial, rolled into one neat package. So I glided through: I woke up at seven every morning, and like every other patient, I was given chores before I participated in the mandatory lectures, group counseling sessions, and one-on-one therapy meetings, too.

I was given reading and writing assignments, designed to make me explore the root of my involvement with drugs. I was impressed with the professionalism and commitment of the Smithers staff, but unconvinced that I belonged there.

This was especially true when I listened to accounts of other patients' lives and addictions. Some would stand up in front of the group and tell of shooting coke and heroin under their tongues to avoid detection. One man said the only needle-free spot on his body was his neck, and didn't think twice about shooting heroin there, either.

When it came time for me to speak, I told the truth: that I used coke once a week at the start, then increased to two to three times a week more recently, and almost always as a way to party with pretty women. Some of the other patients laughed out loud.

"Come on, man. You're lying," one of them said.

I explained to them that I was enrolled in Smithers not because I was an addict, but because I was a recreational user who just happened to violate baseball's drug policy. It was a terrific spin, of course, but utterly wrong. On balance, I learned everything and nothing about addiction. My thick wall of denial was intact. I actually believed that I'd won the war with coke.

In fact, I was so bulletproof that on the very first road trip back with the Mets, I started drinking again. Drinking, because I believed I was stronger than any urge to use coke. And drinking, because all the Mets did, and I wanted to show that I was still one of the boys.

I was so ready to reconquer the world that on June 5, when I returned to the Mets in a start against the Pirates, I considered it the biggest game of my life. I was a little worried about how the fans would react to me, especially because Dick Young wrote in the New York *Post* that before the first pitch, everyone should stand up and boo me.

I didn't understand that. I thought that considering how much I'd meant to the Mets, how much entertainment I'd given baseball fans in New York—and how I'd fought my way back from this brush with coke—I deserved a second chance. Every person deserves this, even a drug user.

Thankfully, the fans at Shea were kinder than Young, because when I was introduced, I heard about 95 percent cheers, with only a smattering of boos. It helped a lot that I beat the Pirates that day, 5–1, which I guess was my way of saying "take that" to Young.

I never really forgave him for the harsh column he wrote. In fact, we never spoke again, since he died later that summer. In the meantime I tried to reclaim my place in the Met landscape, and I tried to put my personal life back in order. I proposed to Monica during my stay at Smithers; she'd proved beyond a shadow of a doubt that she loved me—through good times or bad.

I'd been considering marrying her even before my suspension, but her willingness to put up with my embarrassment, not to mention her willingness to see beyond all the lies I told her that winter about where I'd been—when I was really off getting high with some of my good-time buddies—showed me what a wonderful woman I'd found.

IT WAS SEVEN years before I touched cocaine again, although I never stopped drinking. In fact, I always kept the door slightly open for another fall, because I failed to see the connection between alcohol and drugs. Somehow, for reasons I'll never understand, my addiction remained dormant, and little by little, summer after summer, I began to distance myself from the awful episode in my life.

Major League Baseball kept an eye on me, testing me two to three times a week in 1987 and 1988. But the longer I went without a slipup, the less frequent the tests became. By 1990, I was checked only once or twice a season, and I usually got word that a testing representative would be visiting me a day or two in advance.

Not that I needed the notice: I was clean, although not entirely sober. Despite what I'd learned in Smithers about changing the people, places, and circumstances of my prior drug use, I was still leading a late-night social life, which, over the course of time, robbed the Mets of so much potential greatness.

Even though I missed two months of the '87 season, I still went on to win fifteen games, which I considered respectable enough. But for the first time in my career, my ERA finished higher than

3.00. We ended the season second to the Cardinals in a dramatic race, although injuries to the pitching staff were devastating. At one point or another during that season, all five of our starters were hurt, which explained in part why our win total slipped from 108 in 1986 to 92 in 1987.

Of course, no one wins every year, and the hardest feat in baseball is to repeat as world champions, back-to-back. In some ways, the Mets paid for their excesses and good luck in '86 with that heartbreaking, second-place finish. But we all thought 1988 was going to be our year, myself included.

We ran away with the Eastern Division. In fact, we won thirty-one of our first forty-four games, all but clinching things by June. Still, there was a strange lethargy in the clubhouse: we weren't nearly as explosive or magical as we'd been two years earlier. I'm sure it was a bad omen, but we never, ever regained that sense of invincibility that existed in '86.

Still, it was a fine time to be at Shea. I was 18–9 with a 3.19 ERA, and we ended up winning one hundred regular season games. That September, we were joined by Gregg Jefferies, who was, at the time, the organization's best minor-league prospect, and in Joe McIlvaine's words, a future NL batting champion.

There's no question that Jefferies was a terrific hitter; he finished with a .321 average and proved he was a match for any major league pitcher. But it was also obvious what a baby Jefferies was. He'd been catered to his whole career, first by his father and now by the Mets, who were looking for new superstars to take them into the nineties.

Keith and Gary were getting old, and it was clear to me that Wilpon and Doubleday didn't want me or Darryl to be the team's spokesmen anymore. The reasons were obvious enough: I'd had a fall with drugs, and Darryl was just too unpredictable, despite all the home runs he'd hit since 1983.

We needed a better-looking poster boy, and from a distance,

Jefferies had the perfect résumé. He was polite, skilled, stable, not likely to ever get in trouble. The problem with this buildup, of course, is that Jefferies simply didn't know how to act around older, more hardened players.

Keith and Darryl took an instant dislike to him, as did Roger McDowell, who once sawed all of Jefferies's bats in half. It was wrong to do that, but Gregg brought it on himself, as he insisted that his bats be packed and shipped separately on road trips, as if they were somehow better than everyone else's.

In fact, one time on a getaway from Atlanta, Jefferies made a point of handing his bats to equipment manager Charlie Samuels and instructing, yet again, that they be handled delicately. Jefferies then bolted from the clubhouse to make the team bus to the airport.

Straw decided he'd had enough of Jefferies's self-absorption. He, too, had a bus to catch, but Darryl nevertheless walked across the room, took the bats out of Samuels's hands, and said, "Fuck these things. Fuck 'em."

And with that pronouncement, Strawberry dumped every one of Jefferies's bats in the garbage. We all laughed; making fun of Jefferies was the popular thing to do. But in retrospect, I wish I'd been a better friend to the rookie. Or, at the very least, I regret not taking Gregg aside and telling him there were elements of his personality that irritated people, whether he was aware of it or not.

That's just part of being a veteran. When I was a rookie, I was tutored in locker-room protocol by Mike Torrez and Rusty Staub, two generous guys who went out of their way to make me feel comfortable. In fact, it was Rusty who made me realize that taking responsibility for one's mistakes is part of being a big leaguer. I learned this after an especially bad game in 1984, when I just wasn't in the mood to answer questions from the press. So I left before the reporters entered the clubhouse.

The next day, Rusty told me, "If you're a man, you have to

have the guts to say you screwed up. Not just to me or the guys in this clubhouse—but to the press and to the public. It's the only way anyone will ever respect you." And ever since that day, I've made it my business to make myself available to the press, good game or bad.

But the way the Mets treated Jefferies in 1988 was part of a larger problem. We were no longer the happy, miracle team. We'd become the National League's fat cats, coasting all summer until Jefferies showed up. In fact, Mex told the newspapers that summer that we were "a bunch of Little Leaguers." The only way to rectify that, of course, was to win another World Series, and everyone was feeling great about our chances. And why not? We were facing the Dodgers, who didn't have nearly as much talent as we did, and lost to us ten of the eleven times we faced them that summer. All we had to do was roll over Tommy Lasorda four more times, and we were heading to a classic showdown with the powerhouse A's.

But we never made it. Our crossroads came in Game Four, when we were already leading the series, two games to one. I was pitching the ninth inning with a 4–2 lead, but somehow issued a four-pitch walk to John Shelby leading off. So comes the question of the ages: should Davey have removed me for the hard-throwing Randy Myers?

I don't know if there'll ever be a right way to answer that. I'd devastated the Dodgers for the first eight innings. They were mine, and those last three outs were so close, I could feel them. Even the walk I issued to Shelby offered no hint of a collapse. I still had good velocity and felt like I was in control of the at-bat.

That's why Davey left me in the game, because throughout the year I'd slithered through many similar tight spots. A starting pitcher earns that right over time, and now Davey was repaying me for the strength and courage I'd shown since 1984.

Unfortunately, it was the wrong decision. Mike Scioscia was next, and I assumed that because I'd just walked Shelby on four pitches, he'd be taking a strike. At least that's what conventional, textbook strategy called for. So I threw a get-me-over strike. Which is another way of saying, I delivered a fastball down the middle, at about 85 mph, its sole purpose to get ahead, 0–1, in the count.

Scioscia was ready for that meatball. So ready that he crushed it, sending it into the right-field bullpen. There was a silence at Shea that I can still hear, even today. That's how shocked everyone was. The game was only tied, but that two-run HR was so unexpected and so disheartening, we never really recovered.

In fact, the Dodgers beat us, 5–4, in twelve innings that night, and the next afternoon they overwhelmed Sid Fernandez. L.A. was up 6–0 by the fifth inning, cruising to an easy 7–4 win. Although David Cone pitched brilliantly in Game Six, beating Tim Leary, 5–1, we were no match for Orel Hershiser in Game Seven. We managed just five hits off Hershiser, who had a career year and ended up winning the Cy Young Award.

Ron Darling started for us, and I always respected Ronnie as a big-game pitcher. But we were down 6–0 by the second inning, and our season was over just that quickly. I was actually used in relief in L.A.'s five-run second inning, working on just two days' rest. That's how desperate our situation had become. But there was no solving Hershiser. We were history.

Afterward, in the clubhouse, there were tears of disbelief and a lot of hard feelings. Mostly, there was a sense that we'd let history slip through our fingers. This was the fifth year in which we had a great roster, and we knew there was little to show for it—one World Series ring and too many hangovers.

In fact, I was feeling pretty bitter on the plane ride home. Darryl and I were sitting in the last few rows, thinking about how we blew it. To our utter amazement, we heard some of the players up front calmly discussing their winter plans. Some guys were even laughing. For a moment I thought my ears were lying, because here we were, only hours removed from the most painful series defeat in the club's history, and there were teammates who didn't take it to heart.

I didn't have to walk toward the front of the plane to know who the voices belonged to. At least one was Gary Carter's, which shocked me. He was always a great battery mate, and a very enthusiastic, loyal guy. Maybe this was his way of releasing the frustration, I don't know. But his reaction offended me—and Straw.

In fact, Darryl was in a belligerent mood to begin with, and when he heard guys laughing, he tried to pick a fight with any of them, all of them.

"Bunch of pussies up there," Strawberry said loudly, hoping someone would respond.

". . . better shut their fuckin mouths . . .

". . . anyone got a problem with that? . . ."

No one said a word. They knew better than to get near an angry Strawberry. All that bad feeling on the plane carried over into 1989. Darryl and Keith got into an awful, embarrassing fistfight during Picture Day, when the assembled press corps was able to record it.

Straw learned that Keith had been telling writers that Kevin McReynolds, and not Darryl, deserved the Most Valuable Player award in '88. As it turned out, the Dodgers' Kirk Gibson won it, and Darryl figured that Mex cost him enough votes to knock him out of first place.

The two had been freezing each other out all spring, and the war finally erupted when an unwitting photographer decided to place Darryl and Mex together in the team photo. Darryl said, "I'm not sitting next to any backstabber," and the next thing we knew, punches were flying. Straw walked off the field and, disgusted that the Mets wouldn't renegotiate his contract, just packed up and left camp.

Everywhere, it seems, there were problems. Gary Carter got older and slower, and it appeared his days with the Mets were numbered. And Mex knew he was on his way out the door, too, nodding toward Jefferies one day and, under his breath, saying, "There's no way I want to be part of a team that's building around him."

We finished six games behind the Cubs, and won just eighty-seven games. It was our worst performance since my rookie year, and I had feeling the foundation we'd built in the eighties was starting to dissolve. I suffered the first serious injury of my career, tearing a muscle in the back of my shoulder, which limited me to just 118 innings all year.

In fact, I had to leave in the middle of a game against the Reds on July 1, with a nagging but sharp pain in my arm. I was only twenty-four and had never really had a problem like that. Even though it was just wear and tear—and the injury itself didn't require surgery, just rest, three months on the disabled list—that was one of the reasons we never really rallied.

That disappointing season more or less ended Davey's tenure at Shea. He and Cashen had grown openly hostile to each other; I know Frank was getting tired of the wild and crazy Mets, and wanted Davey to keep us in check. We heard the most petty complaints from the front office, like not enough of us were on the top step of the dugout during the national anthem.

And Johnson was just as disturbed by Frank's constant meddling. In Davey's mind, he'd earned the right to manage the way he wanted, since from 1984 to 1989, we were the most successful team in the Major Leagues.

But Johnson was fired in May 1990, when it was obvious we weren't going anywhere. I remember the way Davey was hustled out of the hotel in Cincinnati, without ever getting a chance to really say good-bye to us. He deserved better and it's a disgrace the Mets still haven't invited him back to Shea to honor the years of success the franchise enjoyed on Davey's watch. He is a good man, and a good manager, and I'm sorry some of the guys—

myself included—took advantage of the honor system that he believed in.

Davey never enforced a curfew, never interfered in our personal lives, never asked for anything except that we be on time and play good, crisp baseball. The rest—the drinking on the planes, the womanizing, even the trash we talked on and off the field and in the newspapers—was our business.

But Davey was also growing more distant from us in the last year or two, spending more time in his office and less mingling with the players. He'd assigned that responsibility to Mex and Gary, but this was no longer their team. Darryl and I were really the nucleus, although Jefferies was still the front office's choice.

But with Hernandez and Carter in decline, Davey was cut off. He also made the tactical mistake of backing Jefferies, when it was clear that Gregg was unpopular in the clubhouse. Johnson not only liked Jefferies, but he thought the kid could play second base on an everyday basis now that Wally Backman had been traded to the Twins in the off-season.

Trouble was, Jefferies couldn't play the infield, at least not second, and certainly not on the faster, turf surfaces. Kevin Elster once said, "He's got the range of a bucket of sand." But Davey refused to bend on that issue and that probably accelerated his demise.

By 1990, the crash was coming. Davey was replaced by Buddy Harrelson, one of the more popular coaches on the staff, but as it turned out, he just wasn't ready to handle managing in a big city. We finished second once again, this time getting edged out by the Pirates, and Buddy didn't even make it through a full year.

That year, 1990, was our first without Hernandez, who moved on to the Indians, and Carter, who was now playing with the Giants. All the old warriors had been phased out. Ray Knight had left after the '86 season. Mitch was traded away, Lenny was with the Phillies, Mookie was with Toronto, and Darryl was on his way to the Dodgers via free agency.

Little by little, they'd been replaced by talented but less inspired players: Jefferies for Backman, Dave Magadan for Hernandez, Kevin McReynolds for Mitchell. Getting John Franco as our closer was a nice bonus, because I always knew he had balls. But Johnny had a bad September, just as we were collapsing.

For me, personally, it was a strange season. I started slowly, still tentative over the arm injury I'd suffered in 1989. In fact, on June 2, I was only 3–5 with a 4.37 ERA. But then my engines clicked. I won sixteen of my last eighteen decisions, leaving me with nineteen wins with two starts left in the season. That same summer, Frank Viola, who came to the Mets from the Twins in 1989, was also pushing for his twentieth victory.

The rap on Viola from the American League was that he was a baby—someone who cared more about his personal won-loss record than the fate of the team. You can spot guys like that a mile away. They pout if they go 0 for 4 or pitch poorly, even though the team may have won. Class guys like Ron Darling and Bob Ojeda never, ever cared about their individual stats, as long as we won.

But I could see Viola was obsessed with getting that twentieth win, maybe because in 1988 he missed winning the Cy Young Award by one vote. For five starts, Viola was stuck at nineteen and he wasn't embarrassed to go to Buddy and ask that I be forced to pitch on three days' rest so that *he* could get another shot at his twentieth.

In all, I got one chance to go from nineteen wins to twenty and I failed. Viola, who failed to get to number twenty in five previous tries, got a final, extra start, which I thought was selfish. Viola did win his twentieth, making him the first twenty-game Met lefty since Jerry Koosman in 1976.

But Viola was just passing through New York; he was gone after the disastrous 1991 season, when we crumbled. We won only seventy-seven games and saw Buddy get fired a week before the season ended. That was really the official end of the Mets' golden era and, for me, the beginning of a different chapter in my professional career.

My last start of the year came on August 22; I threw only five innings, and even though I was beating the Cardinals, 6–0, something was very wrong with my shoulder. As it turned out, I suffered a torn labrum and partial tear of my rotator cuff, and two weeks later underwent surgery to repair it.

That was the first time I'd ever had my arm operated on, and looking back, that marked the end of my dominant, I-dare-you fastball. Every power pitcher lives in fear of blowing out his arm. It's inevitable that, sooner or later, one way or another, your fastball will lost its muscles. Even the great Nolan Ryan, the most durable, hardest-throwing pitcher of his generation, was scuffing the ball in his final years, just to compensate for a drop-off in velocity.

I could accept the fact that I was human, just like every other guy who put on a uniform. But what bothered me is that I believed my injury was hastened by Buddy Harrelson's decision to keep me in a game on April 13 of that year, making me pitch in cold, damp weather, running my pitch count up to close to 130, just to beat the Expos, 2–1.

It was a great game for me, make no mistake. I struck out fourteen and defeated Pedro Martinez, 2–1. But it was only our sixth game of the season, and there's no way I should've been extended that long. I didn't realize it at the time, because I was pumped up with adrenaline, but the conditions were so unfavorable, the next day I literally could not raise my arm high enough to brush my teeth.

That's not to say a pitcher doesn't have soreness after a nine-inning start. He does. He always does. It usually lasts a day and a half and disappears altogether when I throw on the side in between starts. But there was something awful about the way my arm felt after pitching against the Expos. It was a deep, ligament pain, as opposed to routine, muscular soreness. The discomfort lasted for almost a week, and I have to believe that's one of the reasons I eventually tore my rotator cuff.

As much as I liked Buddy personally, he should've known better. He should've looked out for me, instead of getting caught up in a pitchers' duel. I guess Buddy was so intent on proving that he could change the Mets' fortunes—remember, we'd finished second two years in a row—he forgot how long the season really is.

That surgery turned out to be a dark landmark for me. I was 13–7 at the time, and never had another winning season for the Mets. Part of the reason was because the teams I played on from 1992 to 1994 were awful—mystifyingly so, because we had so much on-paper talent. But I was also pitching so poorly, and my arm hurt so much, I seriously considered retiring.

Suddenly baseball was no fun anymore. In fact, I felt like an alien on the '92 Mets, since all my old buddies from the '86 club were just about gone. Instead, we had a new general manager in Al Harazin, who'd been promoted to take over for the retired Frank Cashen. Jeff Torborg replaced Buddy Harrelson after having managed the White Sox; Eddie Murray was at first base, Bobby Bonilla was supposed to make the fans forget about Straw in right field, and Vince Coleman, who used to kill us in St. Louis with all those stolen bases, was now our center fielder.

The starting rotation was even more impressive, in theory. It featured me and Bret Saberhagen, two former Cy Young Award winners, and David Cone, who could've easily won one after going 20–3 in 1988.

So how did we lose? How did the '92 Mets flop so badly? I'll never understand that one. None of us performed the way we expected. Maybe it was because the Mets had spent so heavily on

Bonilla and Coleman, and had traded away their favorite son, Gregg Jefferies, to get Saberhagen. The expectations were more than we were ready for.

Maybe it was the wrong chemistry in the locker room—these players were strangers to New York, and couldn't re-create the love the city had for the Mets from six years earlier. Some reporters thought Harazin wasn't a real GM, just a glorified lawyer trying to make baseball decisions. Others thought Torborg was the wrong type of manager for a New York team, although I totally disagreed with that.

In fact, I thought Jeff did a great job. He was the most prepared and organized man I ever played for. He was the first manager to have hitters' and pitchers' meetings; the opposing team was thoroughly scouted, and before each series, we went over their strengths and weaknesses. So what was wrong with preparation?

The other rap on Torborg was that he was too restrictive; no alcohol on team flights, for instance. Again, it was his team, and as manager, he was allowed to make those rules. I think Jeff was trying to make a point about regaining control of his players, after we'd gone berserk in the eighties. I think some of the rules were more symbolic than anything else, actually. We were grown men; if someone was desperate for a drink, he could've just brought it in his coat or jacket. Believe me, the flights weren't exactly dry.

But the longer the season went on, the more restless we became. Bobby Bo never got comfortable in New York, especially after he told the press they weren't going to wipe that smile off his face. That started a war of its own. Murray didn't speak to the press, period, and those negative vibes just made it tough for everyone to coexist.

I know I didn't help matters much. In that three-year downward spiral, between 1992 and 1994, I won a total of twenty-five games. Nothing seemed to work anymore. Hitters were all over my fastball, I couldn't throw my curveball for a strike, and worst of all, I kept fearing that I was going to injure my shoulder again, this time for good. I remember one day in 1993, after I'd gotten my butt kicked by . . . I don't even remember who. I came into the clubhouse and started to tear it up. I threw chairs, knocked over a table, took a bat to one of the cement pillars. Charlie Samuels, the equipment manager, watched me without uttering a word. His silence said everything about his pity for me.

"What the fuck is wrong with me? Why can't I get anyone out anymore?" I shouted. "I'm quitting. I'm going home. I don't need this shit anymore!"

I was serious. I was serious about returning to Tampa every time I lost. Every athlete knows when he's crashed through the wall of mediocrity. When losing becomes the rule, not the exception, and when it's all too acceptable.

I never wanted to get to that point, where I could accept being a .500 pitcher. Maybe I wasn't ever going to be a 24–4 stud like I was in 1985, but the embarrassment I experienced on opening day in 1994 was, to me, a sign from the gods to find a new job.

That's because I surrendered three home runs to the Cubs' Tuffy Rhodes in Wrigley. I'm man enough to know that every pitcher gets smoked in the big leagues. Even the best get beat up, sometimes badly. But there was no way for me to rationalize those three HRs, hit by someone who I would've devoured in my prime.

After the third HR, I was so angry and embarrassed, I kicked the dugout step hard enough to break my big right toe. What irony: after years of worrying about my arm, it's my toe that sent me to the disabled list and all but ended my association with the Mets. I spent almost six weeks away from the team, and I never felt more removed from baseball.

By 1994, Torborg and Harazin had both already been fired; Cone, who never bought into Torborg's live-clean, always-be-prepared credo, had been traded. Murray couldn't get out of New York fast enough and Coleman was injured so often, he never got to show off his base-stealing skills. In fact, in his two years with the Mets, 1991 and 1992, he missed a total of 180 games. Vince didn't make a great impression at Shea, either.

Even though I liked him personally, he stepped over the line in September 1992, when he actually jostled Torborg on the field, in full view of the fans. It started when Vince had been ejected by umpire Gary Darling for arguing a checked-swing, called third strike. Vince was in Darling's face, since he'd been thrown out by the same crew two nights earlier against the Braves. Torborg interceded, but instead of arguing with Darling, Jeff proceeded to push Vince back toward the dugout. Torborg wasn't crazy about Vince; he thought Vince was too loud and laughed too much, especially after we lost and he was on the disabled list. Jeff was a real rah-rah guy, and Coleman just didn't fit his profile.

So maybe that shove was just Torborg's reflex, trying to save his player from being ejected and suspended. Maybe it was the frustration of a losing season.

Or maybe it was Jeff's way of telling Coleman he was sick of him. In any case, Coleman reacted badly, shouting back, "What the fuck are you pushing me for?" He actually returned Torborg's shove and Bobby Bo alertly hustled Vince off the field. But the damage had been done.

Torborg kept his composure, walking back to the dugout and then waiting for Coleman to head up to the clubhouse. Once Coleman was out of sight, Jeff practically sprinted toward the clubhouse himself, where he confronted Vince. There were a few people in the clubhouse who witnessed it, and they said it was one of the most heated arguments they'd ever seen between a manager and a player.

Jeff demanded an apology and Vince said, "Go fuck yourself." Torborg went right back at him, and said he'd never allow a player to show him up on the field like that, immediately suspending Vince for two games.

There was no question that Vince was wrong in that situation. Clearly wrong. You don't have to like your manager, but physical contact is where you lose the moral high ground. To no one's surprise, Vince was gone in 1993, even though he played out only half of his four-year, $11.65 million contract with the Mets. He was another big-name guy who was just passing through, as the Mets kept looking to re-create that old '86 magic.

What was so sad is that the recipe for the '86 success didn't come from money, or free agents, or managers with breakthrough approaches. It was all about good players who loved baseball. That's all that mattered to us. But what Fred Wilpon and Nelson Doubleday, along with Frank Cashen, never understood is that we won because we were so damn cocky.

Not rich. Not violent. Not stats-obsessed. We just loved to win, and by 1994 the World Series was just a faint memory.

DALLAS GREEN WAS our last-gasp effort for respectability in 1993, having replaced Torborg on May 19. Only six weeks into the season, it was obvious we weren't going anywhere, since we'd lost twenty-five of our first thirty-eight games.

Dallas came to the Mets with a tough-guy reputation. He was supposed to clean up the shabby play on the field and take control of the clubhouse, which, ownership thought, had gotten away from Torborg.

On the outside, I could see where Dallas was a good-looking candidate. He was a former major league pitcher who had a John Wayne presence. He stood six-five with a full head of thick, white hair. He had a deep, booming voice. There was nothing meek about the guy. Dallas had managed the Phillies for two full seasons, 1980 and 1981, and was only the fourth manager in baseball history to win a World Series in his rookie year.

Green also managed the Yankees in 1989, which is probably

why Met ownership thought he could be effective at Shea. But Dallas ran into immediate trouble in the Bronx, as his ego proved to be almost as big as George Steinbrenner's. In fact, he didn't even finish out the year. Green took shots at George in the papers, basically saying Steinbrenner knew nothing about baseball. So Dallas got fired in mid-August, when the Yankees were on a long, flat road to nowhere, just 56–65.

Baseball's gossip network runs across both leagues, so when Dallas's gig was up in the Bronx, we heard some of the inside story over in Flushing. It was true that he was a straight-up guy, but only when the team was winning. People around the Yankees said when things got tight, he blamed his players, especially the young ones. And Green wouldn't think twice about doing so in the papers.

That's a cardinal sin in any clubhouse. Players know the manager carries the weight of the franchise on his shoulders, and he's told he's responsible for many, many things that are out of his control—like the performance of his players, for instance. Most players, the mature ones, anyway, are willing to give their manager a pretty wide berth.

But once a manager starts airing out his players in the press, then it's open season. It's hard enough to succeed in the big leagues—dealing with fans, umpires, and the opposition—without your own manager ganging up on you, too. Ultimately, Dallas saw pretty quickly that the '93 Mets were an awful team, and let everyone know the mess wasn't his doing.

Truth is, we didn't play any better for Green than we did for Torborg; we were 46–78 after May 19, which meant it was a long, ugly summer. The strange thing about Dallas is that I sensed right away he had no particular affection for me, or for the contributions I'd made to the Mets in better days.

Granted, I didn't pitch particularly well for Green: I finished the year under .500, just 12–15, which represented the most games

I'd ever lost in one year with the Mets. But I also thought Dallas went out of his way to embarrass me on July 1, when I was the losing pitcher in a 7–5 loss to the Marlins. I had nothing that day; no fastball, the curveball wasn't sharp, and no location. I was completely naked out there, but Dallas allowed me to get my ass kicked.

Later, when reporters asked Green why he didn't go to the bullpen sooner, he said, "We're paying Gooden a lot of money. He should be giving us a lot of innings."

So that's how he felt—that you measure a pitcher by dollars, not by his velocity or the break on his curveball. It's almost as if Green was punishing me for being the Mets' onetime ace. Now that I was struggling, as we all were, he was in a hurry to push me out the door.

I'm not vain enough to think that I have to strike out every hitter anymore. In fact, I'll be happy just being on the fat side of .500, winning the big games down the stretch and helping my team get into the postseason. As long as I can hold up that end of the bargain, I expect some respect from my manager. But I always felt that Dallas was way too eager to show the world how bad the '93 Mets were, that none of it was his fault. In many instances, he simply stopped managing, just to take the focus away from him.

In the year or so that I played for Green, I came to see that he was a phony. He loved to talk tough, but never, ever backed it up. There were several incidents in the dugout where he would embarrass a player, always a younger player—almost to the point of provocation—but finally, one of Green's victims decided to fight back.

Jeromy Burnitz, an outfielder who was blessed with great speed, made a base-running error, getting thrown out at third base to end the inning. In the dugout, Dallas was all over him, shouting that he was tired of Burnitz's "stupid, fucking mistakes."

Burnitz fired right back at him.

"You don't like it? I'm sick of listening to your shit," he shouted as we scrambled to get in between the two.

Dallas just sneered and said, "You want to settle this one-on-one? My door is always open."

We all wondered how it would play out, since that sounded like a thinly veiled challenge to Burnitz. Of course it was crazy to think of a player actually fighting a manager, especially since Burnitz was twenty-four and Green was sixty. Would Jeromy have actually taken his anger to the next level? We'll never know, because the door to Green's office was closed after the game and remained that way until everyone had left and gone home.

Maybe Dallas was just doing the smart thing, trying to defuse a volatile situation by ignoring it. But it sure punched a huge hole in his tough-guy veneer. After that, no one took Dallas's bellowing quite so seriously anymore.

In fact, in September 1993, after the last game of a disastrous seven-game, Chicago-Houston road trip, Dallas decided he'd seen enough bad baseball.

And now he was going to make a big, loud show of it. One way for a manager to do that is to hold a team meeting and get in our faces. Sometimes that works, but only with the right manager and the right kind of players who respond to it.

Most of the other tactics are just for show, like Dallas's decision that day to turn over the food table in the middle of the clubhouse. That might've looked and sounded impressive—but all it really did was create a terrible mess that the clubhouse kids eventually had to clean up.

I didn't blame Green for losing his cool, actually. We'd lost six of seven on that trip, including all three to Houston. We were in last place in the East, an appalling thirty-eight and a half games out of first place. The game that sent Dallas over the edge, a 7–1 flogging administered by Houston's tough righty Darryl Kile, was just another example of the same, bloodless baseball we'd played all summer.

But what were we, the players, supposed to do? Not eat? Go on a hunger strike? I don't know of a single manager who ever thought his players weren't worthy of food—none, except Dallas Green. "You fucking guys don't deserve this food—none of it," Green roared. He saw all of us at our lockers, with paper plates in our laps, and decided it was time to make a statement: Starve the Mets!

So Green turned over the entire spread. Everything. The table went down in an awful crash, and with it, the food the clubhouse crew had prepared for us. It's part of baseball tradition, that along with laundry service, the staff in the visitors' clubhouse also brings in hot food for postgame consumption. In exchange, players tip the head of the crew an average of fifty dollars for each day they use his services.

Some visitors' clubhouses, like the ones in St. Louis and Philadelphia, always had great food. So did Houston, especially on getaway day—which is exactly the day Green decided to go crazy. Getaway day, the last day of a series, is when the Houston crew would serve chicken-fried steak, my personal favorite in ballpark cuisine.

So when Dallas destroyed the spread, my heart just sank. Now we were out of luck.

Or were we? As I surveyed the carnage on the floor, I noticed Pete Schourek, a young lefthander, doing the exact same thing. He was studying the steak to see if it was still edible.

"Doc, whaddaya think?" Schourek said, quietly enough for Dallas, who was still shouting at the rest of the team.

"I don't know, man," I said. "It'd be a shame to waste that fine food."

Schourek nodded in agreement. No other words were necessary.

We waited until Green was done—as a grand finale, he slapped a full plate right of out Mike Maddux's hands—and then we made our move.

On our hands and knees, without shame or embarrassment, Schourek and I rescued the steak from the floor, loaded up our plates, and enjoyed dinner. And as I found out that day, losing does suck, but nothing diminishes the joy of a good chicken-fried steak.

# FIVE

I'D ALWAYS ENVISIONED playing out my career with the Mets. I couldn't imagine ever leaving the organization, not after all the great times I had at Shea. But after I broke my toe on Opening Day, 1994, I could see that the club was already looking toward a new generation of pitchers—kids like Jason Isringhausen and Bill Pulsipher, who were on their way up from the minors.

I recognized that change is the way of the world, especially in baseball. Loyalty from the club exists only as long as you're young and healthy and winning. I certainly wasn't blind to the manner in which the Mets turned their backs on Keith Hernandez and Gary Carter, two of their most important, dynamic players, when it seemed they were past their primes. But I didn't think I was anywhere near being done. Hell, I was only twenty-eight and the way Dallas talked about me, I could've been fifty.

I guess that's why I was so frustrated at the way Tuffy Rhodes handled me; there was no reason why he should've been able to hit three HRs off me in one game. I knew I was better than that. I just couldn't solve this mystery.

For six weeks, I pondered that on the disabled list. I waited for the toe to heal, which meant all I could do was long-toss in the outfield before games and hang out with my teammates afterward. Actually, by '94, two of my best friends were Steve Garland, the trainer, and Charlie Samuels, the equipment manager. The guys on the team were fine, like John Franco and Bret Saberhagen. I like Bobby Bonilla, too. There were no problems in the clubhouse. But I still hadn't found anyone to replace Straw and David Cone and Ronnie Darling.

Maybe that's why the demon came back for me, after a seven-year sabbatical. Maybe it was the frustration of pitching poorly, or missing the good old days, and worrying that I couldn't get the Tuffy Rhodeses of the world out anymore. All I know is that, without warning, my defenses were lowered.

The real way a recovering addict knows he's in trouble is if he starts thinking about getting high. That means the urge is getting closer, getting stronger. By late May, my broken toe was strong enough for me to begin an injury rehab assignment, which meant every four days, I was scheduled to leave the Mets and pitch for one of their minor-league clubs.

It was at Class AAA Norfolk where I first recognized the signs of a crisis. There, I took note of the fact that a representative from Major League Baseball had not been present to take my urine sample, which, in the last two years, had once again been collected on a strict, three-times-a-week basis.

The absence of a tester ignited the engines of deception. I started to wonder if I could I get away with a line or two. I mean, if the tester didn't show up in Norfolk, perhaps that meant I wouldn't be tested in any minor-league affiliate during my pitching-rehab program.

It was June 2, a Wednesday night, and I was in Manhattan, at a nightclub, drinking heavily. In fact, I was drunk and fast-forwarding to the rehab start I was to make at Class AA Binghamton in two days. According to my hazy logic, if the tester, who didn't show up in Norfolk, didn't make it to Binghamton on Friday, that meant my next test wouldn't be until Monday. And that gave me a five-day window.

Sad, but true: after seven years, I was right back where I started. The more I drank that night, the more tempting it became to get high, especially after I learned that the guy behind the bar had some coke and would be happy to share it with me. Did I want to? Sure I did. Did I think I could get away with it?

At eight P.M., I said no way. By ten, I was open-minded to it. And now, by two A.M., I was ready for the plunge. I said yes, for the same reason a bank robber walks through the front doors of a bank, despite the presence of guards, surveillance cameras, and dozens of potential witnesses. He does it because, somehow, he thinks he's smarter than the system. And that was my downfall, too.

I did six fat lines in the bathroom, getting wonderfully high, experiencing the rush an addict never truly forgets. Everything around me had that surreal, super-fast, but super-calm feeling—like a movie in fast forward while I'm still at regular speed. It was a nice high, and mixed with the alcohol, it kept me insulated from the awful choice I'd made. I went home, went to sleep, and woke up staring at a crisis. The moment I opened my eyes, I asked myself: What the hell did I just do?

I knew that another positive test would mean another suspension from baseball. And considering I was to become a free agent after the season, another relapse would surely sever my ties with the Mets. They would never, ever forgive me a second time.

So why did I get high?

Why?

I spent the next two days worrying, sweating, experiencing an anxiety so intense, I thought I'd pass out, right on the field. I indeed pitched at Binghamton, and just like I thought, the tester never showed up. I took some solace in that. In fact, for a few hours, I thought everything was cool and that I could just resume my baseball life. But during my night of drinking, it never occurred to me that the rep might just show up in Cincinnati, where I was supposed to join the Mets the next day, on Saturday.

Not once did I think that far in advance. When I flew from Binghamton to Cincinnati, my teammates were happy to see me—buddies like John Franco and Todd Hundley. But being in Riverfront Stadium was pure pain, because I was expecting the worst. Within minutes of my arrival, the fates let me know just how stupid I'd been.

"Hey there, Doc . . . how you been?"

It was the tester, friendly and untroubled. He was standing in front me like nothing was wrong.

"This . . . this is Saturday," I stammered. My throat was closing up with fear.

"Yeah, I know, I couldn't make it up to Binghamton yesterday, so I thought I'd get you here and get it over with," he said, still smiling. "Anyway, you ready?"

The tester wanted to get in and out of the ballpark right away—take the urine sample, seal it, and overnight it to the lab in New York for testing. Then he could enjoy his weekend. But I wasn't ready to say yes. In fact, I had no plan, no alibi. Nothing. So I stalled.

"Look, man, I gotta do my running in the outfield. I'm late and Dallas is already pissed off at me," I said. "I'll be back in a few minutes, okay?"

The tester looked mildly disappointed, but relented.

"Sure," he said. "I'll be here."

I practically sprinted out of the clubhouse, up the runway to the dugout, and onto the field. Batting practice hadn't begun yet, and I was practically alone in the empty stadium. Where could I hide? What could I do?

A million scenarios ran through my mind. I thought about running laps around the outfield, with the hope that with enough exercise and sweat, my body would metabolize the drugs. Or else I could just keep running right out of the ballpark, into a cab, to the airport, and home to Tampa. I could say there was a family emergency, that my father was ill, and that I was so traumatized by the news that I didn't even think of coming back to the clubhouse.

Missing the drug test would look bad in the eyes of Major League Baseball, and might even cost me another suspension. But it still couldn't have been any worse than another positive test result.

I thought about asking a teammate to submit the urine sample for me. That would be difficult to do, because the tester would usually accompany me into a private room to observe. But it wouldn't be altogether impossible, not if I had time to think.

I could pretend to become ill—have a heart attack or a seizure, or just collapse on the ground and pass out.

Or else I could simply confront my problem head-on. Like a man. I could accept the responsibility of my actions and let the fates have their way with me. I wished I could hit some rewind button in my life, go back to that Manhattan club three days earlier and walk out the door when the coke was in front of me. It would've been even smarter of me not to get drunk.

But the truth was I knew I was going to use again; for whatever reason, the beast was back and that meant, whether I got away with it this time or the next time, sooner or later I was going to get caught. The revelation hit me like a punch in the face. The only way I could repair the damage would be to meet it squarely, with whatever integrity I could muster.

So I took a deep breath and walked back into the clubhouse. The tester was waiting for me, and as I finished the procedure, I said to myself: What happens, happens. It's out of my hands now.

A FEW TORTUROUSLY long days went by after the test, which both surprised me and raised my hopes. The Mets went on to Florida for a three-game series, and each day, when I heard nothing, I began think perhaps I'd dodged a bullet.

Was it possible that the coke had actually left my system in only three days? Everything I'd ever read and heard about, everything I was ever taught at Smithers, said that was impossible. Yet close to a week elapsed and no one around the Mets seemed to know anything.

Then, finally, my little fantasy came to an end. Dr. Alan Lans met the team in Atlanta, our next stop on the road trip. He was waiting for me when I walked into the clubhouse.

"Doc, you're going to have to come with me to New York," Dr. Lans said gravely. "I don't know exactly what this is about, but I think we have a problem."

My heart sank, and for a moment or two I just stared at the floor. I'd been caught. It was over. I knew Dr. Lans was trying to soften the blow, saying he wasn't entirely sure why I was being summoned to New York. But he knew exactly, and he was just trying to be kind to me.

I know my positive test must've been a huge disappointment to Dr. Lans; he was a good guy who did his best for me. I told him, "There must be a mistake. I didn't use. There's got to be something wrong here."

Dr. Lans's answer was a sad, droopy smile. There wasn't much he could say, since the matter was no longer in his hands. Together, he and I flew to New York, where we met with Lou Melendez, the associate counsel of the Player Relations Committee. That's

Major League Baseball's administrative arm, and it was their job to enforce and oversee my after-care program.

Melendez slid a piece of paper across the table to me, the one I signed back in 1987 agreeing to the terms of my first suspension. It said that if I ever tested positive again, I would be subject to an immediate sixty-day suspension.

Even until this last moment I was wondering if there was a way out. But not this time. The test, they said, had been rechecked several times, at more than one laboratory. I guess that was the delay. I was supposed to begin my suspension immediately, they said, although, for now, their recommendation was for increased testing. No rehab. Not at this point. But first, the Mets wanted me to pitch that night against the Pirates.

I blinked once, then twice, wondering if I'd heard them correctly. I looked at Dr. Lans, then at Melendez, at Drs. Millman and Solomon, who consulted in such matters for MLB and the Players Association. It was the Mets' wish, they said, that I take the mound. Only after the game would the announcement be made that I'd been suspended.

Why would the Mets want me to pitch when they knew of my positive test? Were they so concerned about spin control that they figured an after-game announcement would be too late for many newspapers' editions—and that way, the news's impact would be diminished? Were the Mets more concerned about me or the way it would make them look?

In retrospect, I should've refused to take the ball. Was pitching a great game going to change anything? Reduce the length of my suspension? Get me reinstated? Of course not. Hell, I should've just packed my things and gone right home, let the Mets do all the explaining. Better yet, I should have held my own press conference before the game, about an hour before the first pitch, and said, "I've got a drug problem, but the Mets won't let me take care of it. Not until I go out there and pitch."

But I didn't do any of those things. To the end, I played the role of the good guy, and of course I suffered because of it. I got my ass kicked by the Pirates. My mind was elsewhere from the very first pitch, wondering how I was possibly going to explain this second fall to Monica, my kids, the public, and worst of all, my parents. I couldn't even imagine the heartache my father was going to feel.

I tried to at least give some of my teammates the courtesy of telling them before the game. I didn't want them to find out from the press. I spoke privately with Bret Saberhagen and John Franco, two guys I knew I could trust. And, of course, Charlie Samuels, who'd been so loyal to me from the start. And Dallas obviously knew. I got knocked out of the game in the fifth inning, giving up six runs, including two home runs to Dave Clark. I couldn't wait for it to be over, so I could get dressed, get the hell out of Shea, and get on with my life, however messed up it appeared to be.

I was in the clubhouse putting on my street clothes when Dallas said, "Doc, do what you have to do. Make sure you take care of your family. You've been through this before; they're the ones who are going to suffer with you."

I was actually touched by Green's words, because for one, honest moment, I think he truly let his fake, tough-guy guard down. But, as I found out later, that emotion was either fake or fleeting. Dallas told reporters afterward that he didn't feel sorry for me, because I'd let the Mets down. As if I hadn't shot an arrow right through my family's heart. Nope, it was more important for Dallas to take one last swipe at me.

I can't say that I was disappointed when Dallas was eventually fired by the Mets in 1996, replaced by Bobby Valentine. Green never did have a bag of magic tricks, after all. He ended up being no better than Jeff Torborg, and in fact, a lot less sincere. Finally, it seems, the Mets made a great choice in promoting Valentine from Class AAA, and I'm sure the front office's only regret about Valentine is that he wasn't around sooner.

As for me, the drive from Shea to Roslyn was pure torture. Once again, I was thinking of some slick way to tell my wife that I'd tested positive, got caught, and was out of baseball. Again. How do you tell your wife that you've failed for the second time in the most important aspect of recovery?

It'd be close to impossible to ask for forgiveness; that works only once. In fact, it occurred to me that Monica would be within her rights to pack up and go home to Tampa. She had, indeed, made a wedding vow to stick with me for better or for worse, but I'm sure she didn't count on being married to a two-time drug user.

Driving over the Triboro Bridge, I was consumed by two questions:

How do I explain this?

And, what happens to me now?

The answer, I decided, would come to me only after a few beers, which is why I stopped at a grocery store close to our house, picked up a six-pack, and drank as much as I could, as fast as I could, until I had a pleasant buzz. Then I gathered myself and walked through the front door.

The moment Monica saw me, her eyes became billboards of shock.

"Dwight, what are you doing home? Isn't the game still going on?"

"Yeah," I said, before blurting out, "Mon, I'm in some trouble. I had a positive test again."

At first, she didn't believe me. In fact, my wife actually laughed.

"Don't be fooling around," she said, grinning. "Be serious. Why are you home so early?"

I didn't say a word. I just stared at her, my eyes moistening.

That's when it dawned on her that I was telling the truth. She hugged me, and I held on as tight as I could, hoping to squeeze all the demons right out of me.

THE NEXT MORNING I picked up the phone and made the most difficult phone call of my life.

"Mom," I said. "It's me."

"Dwight, is there something wrong? There is, isn't there?"

Once again, my mother's crisis detector was working perfectly.

"Mom, they're going to suspend me again," I said grimly. I tensed up and added, "I missed a test and now they're going to punish me for it."

Of course, that was a naked lie, but at the moment it came to confessing, I couldn't break her heart again. And I hadn't even spoken to my father yet. Was I really wrong to try to sugarcoat this awful occurrence in my life?

Well, maybe I was well intentioned, but my little white lie evaporated in front of my mother, who knew instantly I wasn't telling the truth.

"Dwight, it has to be more than just missing a test," she said. "They wouldn't do this to you just for missing a test."

By now, my father, who was in the other room, must've sensed something wrong, just from the tone in my mother's voice. He took the phone and asked what was the matter.

"Dad, I don't know how to tell you this, but I'm going to have to miss some time again," I said. "I slipped up. I might have to go get some help."

I clenched the phone and prepared for the worst, whether it was anger or silence or that awful sound a receiver makes in your ear when someone hangs up on you. I was shocked, however, to hear my father actually offer me that kind of advice a troubled son so desperately needs.

"You've got to take care of yourself. It's time to be a man about this," my dad said. "You have kids, you have a family. Your life comes first now, not baseball."

For my father to have actually said that . . . well, his sentiments just blew me away. That was the first time in my life I ever heard him say that baseball came second, to anything. That list included school, work, relationships, even my love for them, my parents, I suspected. But my parents must've obviously feared for me, and I can't say I blamed them.

They knew I'd been pitching poorly, playing on a bad team, getting little or no enjoyment out of baseball anymore. My glory days were long over, it seemed. Facing a long, frustrating stay on the disabled list, I turned back to cocaine.

No wonder my father begged me to get help. I sure as hell needed it.

For the next three days I stayed in New York, a prisoner in my own house. I didn't want to leave, because to do that would've meant I'd have to face the press and answer questions I had no answers to.

Why did I get high again? What's going to happen to my career? Are you a hopeless addict?

I didn't know. I didn't know. I didn't know.

What was certain, however, was that news of my suspension was all over the newspapers and television, and somehow I'd have to explain it all to my kids. I told my eight-year-old son, Dwight Jr., that I needed a little help to fix a problem, and that I'd be gone for a month.

"The problem is drugs. I just wanted you to know about it first from me," I said.

Dwight nodded and said he understood, which simultaneously comforted and crushed me. Dealing with my daughters, Ashley, who was four, and Ariel, who wasn't even three yet, was obviously easier. I just said I was going on a road trip, and that I'd be home soon.

Then, out of nowhere, Ashley asked, "Dad, you ever been to jail before?"

"Jail?" I said, so stunned I could only repeat the question.

"Some girl said you were in jail once," she said.

I half smiled and said I'd never been in prison, but that the police took me to the police station once. I'm not sure Ashley understood the difference, but I didn't press the point. Instead, I wondered if this was the legacy I was leaving my children.

## MAY 14, 1996 (CONTINUED)

I WAS SITTING at my locker, still about two hours before game time, and realized no one was talking to me. It's not unusual for a starting pitcher to be off in his own world, but the isolation I was feeling was more intense than that.

My teammates were deliberately avoiding me. I knew why: it was obvious that my thoughts were with my father, and guys figured the best thing to do was to let me sort this out by myself. Kenny Rogers, one of the kindest, gentlest people I've ever met in my career, stopped by for a second, tapped me on the shoulder, and said, "Hang in there, bro." I appreciated the gesture, but I knew I wasn't about to get any meaningful counseling in that clubhouse.

Athletes speak to each other in a macho shorthand, which we learn as far back as Little League—when being tough means never showing too much emotion. Where "hang in there" really means "I know what you're going through, and if there's anything I can do to help, just tell me. I love you like a brother." That's what Rogers wanted to say, or what he meant to say. But the best he could do was, Hang in There.

Actually, Kenny was far more verbal than some of the other

Yankees—which wasn't to say they didn't care. Quite the opposite: they were trying to be so considerate, no one wanted to say that wrong thing. And for many of them, that meant taking the safest route possible, which was to say nothing.

I guess that's why I walked back into Torre's office, which was empty now. He and the rest of the staff were already on the field for batting practice. As a starting pitcher, I was on my own; if I wanted to hang out in the dugout, or shag fly balls in the outfield, or just watch TV in the clubhouse, it was my choice.

So no one was around when I finally called Monica, who'd been waiting all day for me to make a decision about returning home. She was at the house, and I know how anxious she was, because the phone didn't even ring once before she picked it up.

"Dwight?" she said.

"Mon, it's me," I answered. "I'm staying."

"You're what?" she said. In just those two words, I could hear her disapproval, but I'd made up my mind, and I wasn't about to argue now.

"This is something I'm going to do. It's something I have to do," I said.

There was a silence on the phone, which means she went from disagreeing with me to getting angry. But the door was closed on any discussion.

"Dad would understand. I guarantee you if he could speak right now, he'd say the right thing was for me to pitch. So I'm pitching. I'll see you first thing tomorrow morning."

I put the phone down, and prayed that I'd made the right choice. But as I told Monica, there was no turning back now.

As I walked out of Joe's office, I was shocked to realize I was no longer tired, and the buzzing in my head, the pain in my eye sockets—it'd all disappeared. They'd been subdued by an athlete's purest drug, adrenaline.

Ask any athlete, and he'll tell you there's no greater rush than the one that you feel in the last few moments before a big game. Your heart goes off on a sprint, your breathing becomes shallow, and you practically exist outside of your body. The thought of facing the Mariners, coupled with fear of losing my dad, had sent me somewhere I'd never been to before. To this day, I still don't know what happened in the first six innings of that game.

The memory is like some long blur in my mind, cut by only a few sharp images. I remember stepping onto the field, hearing the crowd roar. I don't remember hearing the national anthem, or taking my warm-ups or even that the crowd—over thirty-one thousand—was unusually large for a chilly midweek night in May.

But I do still see this: a 3–2 curveball that I threw on the outside corner to leadoff hitter Darren Bragg that I thought could've been called a strike. Home-plate umpire Dan Morrison squeezed me a little, however, and I'd committed a cardinal baseball sin, which is walking the leadoff man. That's true in any game, any circumstance, any inning, but against the Mariners, that's like typing out your own death wish, because just behind Bragg in the batting order was Alex Rodriguez.

He was only twenty years old at the time, but I knew this kid could hurt me. Rodriguez had enormous power for someone so young. I'm not just talking about weight-room power. Rodriguez poses a threat to pitchers because his swing is so quick and he has so few holes to exploit.

I had a pretty good fastball that night—even in walking Bragg, I could feel its life—and I figured I would challenge Rodriguez. I still wasn't sure I could pinpoint my curveball, not at that point, so I needed strikes. What also factored into my thinking was that Griffey was on deck, and as much as I hated facing Rodriguez with a runner on, it'd be even more threatening to have to deal with Junior with two runners on.

That was smart, textbook thinking, but what I didn't count on was Rodriguez being so locked into a fastball that I'd wanted over the outside corner. Joe Girardi had put his glove right on the black, as far outside as we could possibly aim and still get a strike call. But the fastball had so much last-second movement, it tailed back toward the middle of the plate, which is exactly what Rodriguez was hoping for.

To say he hit it well was an understatement: he smoked it, and my first thought as it went screaming to right center was that no one would catch it. I turned and saw Gerald Williams turn once, then turn around again, which meant he was in trouble.

Normally, Gerald would've never been in center, except that Bernie Williams—the most graceful outfielder I'd seen in years—was on the bench with an injury. How ironic that Gerald was in hot pursuit of Rodriguez's blast, because Gerald always made a habit of approaching before my starts and, with a devilish little smile, say, "Doc, you're going to throw a no-hitter today." That was his way of wishing me good luck.

I didn't know much about Gerald before I signed with the Yankees—I'd only heard that he was arrogant, tough to deal with, unapproachable. That reputation couldn't have been more inaccurate. Gerald was a sincere guy who kept to himself—loyal to the friends he allowed in—and above all, he loved baseball.

Loved it, and practically mastered the art of outfield brilliance. Gerald was a little faster than Bernie, and his instincts, right at impact, might've been a step quicker. But Gerald was a left fielder by trade, and when I saw him change directions on Rodriguez's blast, I thought, not even Gerald's speed was going to help.

But then a small miracle took place in front of my eyes. At the very last moment, with the ball seemingly still on the rise, and Gerald on a full sprint toward the warning track, he reached up and caught it.

Caught it, with half the ball sticking out of the top of his glove.

Caught it, turned, and fired a long, perfect strike to Derek Jeter, who was acting as the cutoff man behind second base.

Caught it, and started a stunning double play, getting Bragg—who never imagined Gerald could make up so much ground so fast.

Jeter wheeled and fired a one-bounce strike to Tino Martinez, beating Bragg by four full steps. The crowd went crazy, and when I got out of the inning without giving up any runs, I wanted very much to tell Gerald how much his play meant to me—that I was playing for a greater purpose than just winning one game in May.

Instead, all I did was wait for Gerald at the top step of the dugout, high-five him, and tell him, "Nice play."

Fluent macho shorthand.

Listening to two voices of experience and wisdom, Joe DiMaggio and Yankees VP Arthur Richman, in spring training, 1996

With Ray Negron, who couldn't understand why I struggled in spring training, 1996. I knew it was just a matter of time, though.

With Steve Howe. Like me, he fought his demons, every day.

With Ray, after another bad outing in spring training, 1996

Darryl Strawberry and Ray, spring training, 1996

Bernie Williams and Derek Jeter, full-time baseball stars, part-time charter flight musicians

The Yankees charters were sure quieter than the Mets charters.

With Team Mariano—Duncan and Rivera, two big reasons why we won it all in '96

Jorge Posada and Ramiro Mendoza, good-naturedly suffering through rookie hazing. We took their clothes and forced them to travel with these ridiculous outfits.

Chatting with MTV's Downtown Julie Brown in 1990

Jeff Nelson about to give Kenny Rogers a hotfoot in the bullpen

Messing around with Yankee left-hander Graeme Lloyd

My buddies Ray Negron and Vincent Kenyon

The price you pay for drug relapses: closely monitored testing by Major League Baseball

I can still hear my dad: Push off the back leg, keep the arm up, follow through.

Two kids with great futures.
Or so we thought.

With George Clooney, along with Ray and Yankee trainer Steve Donahue, when I paid a visit to the Warner Bros. studios in 1997. Warners bought the rights to my life story after the no-hitter and was developing a script for a feature-length movie.

My teacher and friend,
Mel Stottlemyre

With Vera Clemente, wife of the late, great Pirates outfielder, running a kid's clinic in San Juan while I played in the Puerto Rican winter league. This was right after I signed with the Yankees in October 1995.

Ron Dock, that skinny, tough ex-Marine who helped save my life

With Vera Clemente, at the Clemente Sports Complex in San Juan

Me and Reggie Jackson receiving an award for our work with kids in spring training

Me and the Boss, on opposite sides of the fence, but still friends

PART II

# DARK DAYS

# SIX

ON JUNE 24, 1994, the Mets released a statement which they said had been written by me. It read: "I have been suspended for breaking the rules of my aftercare program. I'm truly sorry it happened. I want to apologize to the club, my teammates and the people of New York City. I want to thank everyone for their loyal support. I will be back stronger and better. I want to earn your respect back."

That, of course, was pure spin. I didn't write a word of it, nor was I in the mood to thank anyone for anything. Actually, I felt like I could've taken a pistol and put a bullet in my brain, which is why the Mets probably decided it'd be a good idea for me and the family to return to St. Pete. Away from the intense scrutiny of the New York media, I'd be able to collect my thoughts, get my life together, and who knew, maybe find a way out of this mess.

So on July 1, we all boarded a plane to Florida, where I found

. . . nothing. I had escaped into the great emptiness. I'd forgotten how oppressively hot St. Pete could be in the middle of the summer, and without any baseball to look forward to, I found the days to be endless. This was my first taste of a real-life unemployment—the heavy, unrelenting sense of boredom and frustration that brings a jobless man to his knees.

I didn't even want to get out of bed in the mornings. What was there to do? By nine A.M. it was already too steamy to go for a run, and I sure wasn't playing ball. Even if I did walk around a mall, did I really want to pretend I didn't see the stares and hear the side-of-the-mouth comments from my neighbors? Even the small talk from the well-intentioned ones?

The wide-screen TV in my house offered some refuge, but every time I clicked on the remote, there was another baseball game. I couldn't bring myself to watch—especially when the Mets were on. That was my world, my job, my sport, all of it beyond my reach now.

For three days I lived with this self-inflicted pain. Monica tried to help, being as kind as she could, but my misery was ultimately more then she could understand. By July 4, when I accepted an invitation to a cookout in the neighborhood, I found myself staring at a cold beer, wondering: Why Not? What was stopping me from enjoying it? From having six or seven of them? What was the difference if I sat down with a full case of beer and just polished it off, right then and there?

It's not like I had a game to pitch that night, or the next, or anytime in the foreseeable future. So I popped the top, and there I went—a long, slippery slope downhill. I got wasted in record time, since I hadn't had anything to drink in over a month. And as if I was on some kind of automatic pilot, I got in my Mercedes, drove over the Howard Frankland Bridge into Tampa, and got high again that night.

There was nothing stopping me now. For the next three weeks,

I was drunk every night, getting high without restraint. I was depressed and out of control, especially at night. I couldn't stop drinking and using. I came home so late Monica wouldn't even see me walking in the house.

This whole time, Major League Baseball kept testing me, and the results told the story of my decline. There was one time after I'd used when I called Dr. Lans and asked if there was any point in submitting to the test; I knew it'd come up dirty. He told me to go ahead, which only strengthened MLB's resolve to get me into a rehab program.

There was no saying no. I had to go, if there was to be any chance of a reinstatement in 1994. But this time I wasn't going to Smithers. Instead, I was off to the Betty Ford Clinic in Palm Springs, California—a much more glamorous and expensive facility. It had treated some of the biggest celebrities in America, including Mickey Mantle, who would become a patient there in 1995.

For the next twenty-eight days, I was clean, completely separated from the beast. Not that I had much choice, sequestered at Betty Ford. But I made the best of my time there. I must say, it's truly a beautiful facility, staffed by intelligent, caring people who know their stuff. Just like at Smithers, the people at Betty Ford directed me toward a set of daily chores, required me to attend group and one-on-one sessions, encouraged me to write about my experiences with drugs, and generally explore every avenue of my addiction.

It wasn't hard to be away from cocaine because, for one, I was in a totally sterile environment. By that I meant, there were no "friends" who were offering me drugs, no parties to attend, and most importantly, no alcohol. If there was one thing I'd come to learn about my relapses, it's that they occurred only after I'd been drinking, and specifically, scotch or whiskey or a dark-colored liquor.

I never had a problem when I was under the influence of beer or gin or vodka. I'm not sure I understood why, and I have never presumed that had I stayed off the darker-colored liquors I would've never succumbed to coke. All I did, it seems, was just make it easier to fall down again.

As in any legitimate rehab program, the people at Betty Ford made it clear they weren't miracle workers. They couldn't guarantee that I'd beat my addiction, and they sure couldn't offer me a magic pill to suppress the urge to use.

Instead, they gave me the tools to fight cocaine once I returned to the real world. And, really, that's all I could've expected: to be better informed, to be better prepared, to know how to respond the next time I felt the pull toward the dark side.

For instance, the doctors put me in touch with local chapters of Alcoholics Anonymous, and insisted that I attend ninety straight meetings in the first ninety days after my release—just to reinforce the lessons I'd learned. They said it was important to find a sponsor, someone to act as a personal guide through this maze. Someone who'd been there before and, like me, was struggling to stay clean and sober, twenty-four hours at a time.

And finally, I was told to strengthen my ties at home. Not that I needed any clarity on that issue, but the Betty Ford people wanted me to understand that, sometimes, the best life preserver can be a parent or a cousin or, very often, a wife.

They were right about that much. During the month I was away, I came to realize just how deeply Monica was committed to our marriage. She was six months' pregnant with our son Devon, yet every weekend she'd fly cross-country into Los Angeles, then take a commuter flight to Palm Springs just to visit me and be part of the Family Day activities.

There was no way I could begin to thank Monica for her understanding and her commitment to me. I saw that she intended to stick it out, even though I'd put her through some great hardships, both physical and emotional. In fact, there were moments when I fully expected to call home and discover that she'd left. I can't say that I would've blamed her, or that if the tables were turned, I could guarantee I'd have the same perseverance.

Yet there she was, upbeat and loving, determined to see me through this battle. Unfortunately, the war was far from over, even after such intensive treatment. No matter how many times I listened to the doctors and counselors, who urged me to accept my addiction and fight it head-on, a part of me was still in denial.

I still thought that I was on top of my drug problem. In fact, I remained unconvinced that I had any "problem" at all—that all I'd had was a onetime slipup, which was corrected easily enough. Although I respected Betty Ford's program and their well-intentioned staff, I would've never agreed to enter unless I'd been directed to by Major League Baseball.

In fact, I'd been thinking of ways to return to the Mets after my sixty days were up, but the Players Association called a strike on August 12, when I was just fourteen days short of reinstatement. Even though I wasn't technically on an active roster, the owners still considered me a striking player; therefore I'd have to wait until the labor dispute was resolved to complete my time.

That meant I was officially out of a job, and the day I walked out of Betty Ford, I was staring at a completely empty horizon: no baseball, no salary, no responsibilities. At least I got the chance to meet up with Darryl Strawberry when I left the clinic. In fact, Darryl and his new wife, Charisse, picked up me and Monica up at the front door and took us to their home in nearby Rancho Mirage.

It'd been a long time since I'd seen Straw, and a lot had happened to us both. Since leaving the Mets, he'd signed with the Dodgers in 1991, where he had a pretty good first year. He batted .265 with twenty-eight HRs and ninety-nine RBIs. For a brief time Straw sure made the Mets look bad by letting him get away. But then came a series of setbacks, starting with a serious back injury in 1992. Over the next two years with L.A., Darryl played in a total of just seventy-five games, and the depression that followed led him into a serious drug problem. It's hard for me to say whether Darryl was an addict in his Met days; I only know that he used. But by his own admission, he was in deep by '92.

I know Darryl was under a lot of pressure in L.A.; they signed him to a $20.25 million contract through 1995, and after the Dodgers got Eric Davis, Darryl's childhood buddy, the two were expected to make L.A. the powerhouse in the West. But it never happened that way; Darryl underwent back surgery in September 1992, which pretty much wiped him out for '93, too.

What compounded his problem was the ugly and expensive breakup of his marriage to Lisa. That, and the fact that Darryl never got along with Tommy Lasorda, who was one of those managers players either loved or considered a total fake. At one point in '92, Lasorda called Darryl a "dog," which obviously meant their relationship was totally fractured.

Darryl made some bad decisions along the way. In April 1993, he scuffled with a homeless couple he had tried to help. In June that year he was fined $20,000, a day's pay, for showing up late to a game.

All this led to Lasorda calling Darryl into his office on the last day of spring training in '94. Tommy told him, "You've got to get going this year. We're depending on you. We're paying you a lot of money."

Straw subsequently told me that something finally broke inside of him, that he was tired of listening to Lasorda and his phony motivational tactics. But instead of becoming deaf to the man, as so many Dodgers had done over the years, Darryl flipped out. He disappeared for three full days.

I remember hearing the news that he was missing, and I said to Monica, "I just pray Darryl's not dead." I wouldn't have been surprised if something awful had happened to him, at least not then, when he was so deeply involved with drugs.

As it turned out, Darryl finally surfaced, although he never actually told anyone where he'd been. But Straw did confess his drug problem to the Dodgers, who promptly put him on the DL, and entered him into the Betty Ford clinic. The Dodgers released him soon afterward, but to his credit, Straw straightened himself out long enough to hook on with the Giants later that summer.

Darryl didn't put up breathtaking numbers, just .239, four HRs, and seventeen RBIs in ninety-two at-bats—but the Giants saw enough to sign him to a contract for 1995. But like everyone else in baseball, Darryl was home in late August, honoring a picket line that would eventually cancel the World Series.

That meant Straw had plenty of free time on his hands on August 20, which is why I was able to spend the day at his home. Monica and Charisse hung out in the kitchen while me and Darryl walked out by the tennis court.

It was a beautiful, ranch-style home, and I could tell Darryl took pride in it. He had this calm about him now, which I could understand. After all, he had a career again, a wife he loved, and a sense that he was on the right track.

"Doc, you've got to get out of Florida," he said. Darryl never did like my friends in Tampa; it wasn't the first time he offered this advice. We were sitting near his pool when he looked me straight in the eye and said, "Those people around you are killing you."

I nodded. He was both right and wrong. It's true, the key to recovery is to change the people, places, and things that helped bring you down. But you can't run from yourself. I could've done what Darryl had done, fled to the desert, hundreds of miles from the nearest party. But sooner or later you still fight the same internal war. If you're going to use, you'll use, no matter what your zip code.

The two of us spent hours sitting on his porch, reliving the old days. We talked about how we could've done so much more with our careers, how the Mets wasted at least three great seasons—1985, 1987, and 1988—when we should've made it to the World Series. And, mostly, we talked about the people we'd lied to and hurt, especially our families.

We went to an NA meeting that night, which felt good. I needed to cement the messages of Betty Ford one more time before I left California, although I had no illusions about the road ahead of me. The next day, when it was time to return to Florida, Darryl and I vowed to stay in touch during the off-season.

And who knew, maybe we could be teammates again. If Darryl was going back to San Francisco, it wasn't impossible for me to think of playing for Dusty Baker, too. After all, the Mets hadn't said a word to me in the last month. Even before the strike, there'd been no mention of me rejoining them in 1994. I was guessing my association with them was over, even though, technically, I was still in their employ.

In fact, I flew back to New York from Betty Ford, where I met with Lou Melendez, and Drs. Solomon and Millman and Dr. Lans. We all agreed I had the weapons to move forward, stay clean, and get back to the big leagues as soon as possible.

"Good luck," Melendez said, shaking my hand,

I thanked him, got on a plane to Tampa—and relapsed that very night.

LOOKING BACK, I realize all the information I'd absorbed at Betty Ford went right through me. I learned everything, and nothing, thinking I was in control of my addiction. I was in denial, blind and stupid, and about to destroy the very foundation of my career, not to mention my marriage.

Why? How? I only wish I'd known then what I know now—

or, to be more precise, I wish I'd been more honest with myself. I still likened addiction to a cold or flu, an affliction that crops up but can be defeated with onetime treatment from a doctor.

You never win. You never stop fighting. An addict is an addict every day of his life, forever. But it would be a while before I met face-to-face with that truth.

When I got home, I told Monica I was going out to see some friends; she seemed to understand and, in fact, encouraged me to get out some. I'd been locked away for a month, and needed to reacquaint myself with the outside world. What I didn't tell her, of course, was that I was going to a club, where these "friends" I'd see were also into heavy drinking.

Still, I don't blame anyone, or anything. It wasn't my "friends" who ordered up three beers, lined them in a neat little row, and chugged right through them. It wasn't my "friends" who loved that wonderful buzz that ensued. And it sure wasn't my "friends" who approached a known dealer who was hanging out near the bar.

I was responsible for every single mistake I made that night. I wanted to show everyone that things were cool with Doc—that even though he'd been in rehab, he was still a good-time guy, still telling funny baseball stories, still the most charismatic person in the club. Of course, for me to handle these self-created responsibilities, I had to seek alcohol's charm, and once I was drunk, it was an easy crossover to cocaine.

The dealer who I saw knew exactly who I was, and like any professional trafficker, he didn't make the first move. He waited until I came to him.

"Whaddaya have?" I slurred.

"Come see me in the bathroom," he said coolly.

Of course, the dealer couldn't have cared less that I'd been in rehab, or that he was acting as a catalyst to my addiction. In fact, it would be a badge of honor for him to tell his colleagues the next day that it was him—and his drugs, his profound sense of style and cool—that went right up the great Dwight Gooden's nose last night in Tampa.

I could almost hear the dialogue now:

"Dwight—Mr. Betty Ford I'm Better Than You Now, I'm Never Touching the Shit Again—Gooden came to see me. And you know what? The motherfucker couldn't wait to go down. He came to *me*. He picked *me*. And I am *honored*."

It's a sick logic, but I couldn't blame him. In the eyes of the dealers, I was a trophy and I played right into their hands. Yes, I did go into the bathroom and allowed the dealer to sell me enough coke to guarantee a great high. The transaction was seamless; no one saw, no one knew.

I walked out of the bathroom feeling bulletproof, although I didn't want my friends to see that I'd just scored. Instead, I pretended to be overtired and said I was calling it a night. One of my friends merely asked if I was okay to drive. I said I was.

The other one, however, knew me better than that. He knew I wouldn't leave a club so abruptly, not when we'd been having such a great time. He knew I must've had a new agenda. "Doc, you okay?" he said. Only, he wasn't asking. He looked straight through me, his eyes acting like accusers. Was my lust for drugs that obvious? I said I was fine, that I just wanted to get home to Monica—it *was* my first night back, after all—but that must've sounded so empty. He just shook his head as I walked out the door.

I got in my car and started driving. With one hand on the wheel, I snorted about two grams of cocaine, about $150 worth. It's obviously dangerous to be using drugs while operating a moving vehicle, but that was part of the thrill. Plus, I always felt that if I pulled over to the side of the road, I became more of a target to police than if I was constantly on the move.

And so I wandered the streets of Tampa in my Mercedes. Driving, and snorting and listening to music, just letting the drug hold me in its embrace. I was very, very high, utterly powerless now to fight my addiction. It seemed the harder I tried to reclaim my life, the more precipitous was my fall. Even through this cocaine haze, I knew I was on the edge, teetering toward a monstrous relapse. Not just today and tomorrow, but in the coming weeks and months, with no end in sight. I didn't bother thinking about an emergency plan.

There was none.

After a few hours I finally came home. Monica was already asleep, so I was thankful she didn't see how messed up I was. Nor did I want her to discover the unused coke that I still had in my possession, which is why, the moment I walked through the front door, I went right to the bathroom and flushed the drugs down the toilet.

That's an expensive practice, I know. I once estimated that in all my years of drug use, I must've deposited at least $50,000 worth into Tampa's sewage systems—because I was either consumed with post-use guilt, or I was paranoid about getting caught.

Even in my very first relapse after Betty Ford, I could sense that something was different. Unlike 1987, when I used coke to be around friends, to enhance my social skills, this time I only wanted to be alone when I was high.

It wasn't a happy feeling. The moment I started to sober up, as I finally pointed my car toward my home in St. Petersburg, I regretted what I did. I asked myself why I bothered, if it was really worth it. If I wanted to start living my life like this.

The answers, of course, were easy to come to: no, no, and no.

But that doesn't mean I was able to stay clean.

In fact, I was entering the worst period of my life—a vicious cycle of drinking, getting high, driving too fast, feeling guilty afterward, and then trying to stay sober for a few days. Inevitably, though, the cycle would start again.

This went on for almost two months. The more I used, the

worse I felt. And the worse I felt, the more self-destructive I became. I was actually fine during the day. It was at night that I was drawn back to Tampa, like some vampire. I'd tell Monica that I was going out to see friends, and then I wouldn't be back until the next morning.

I drank three times a week, four times, sometimes three or four nights in a row. Then I would stop. Sometimes I would drink and not use coke. Sometimes I'd drink and use coke once a week, twice a week. I lost track of my relapses.

The worst part about being an addict is that you lie all the time. You lie to your family, your friends, and, of course, yourself. But it's indefensible when you hurt your loved ones. I remember on September 1, my daughter Ariel was having her birthday party at the house. She was turning four, and Monica had invited all her friends, people from the neighborhood, and of course, our family.

We'd planned this affair for weeks, because we wanted it to be special. Everything was catered, the house was decorated, and the kids would be staying all day long. Everything was in place, except for me, the proud papa, who wasn't around.

Where was he? Too high to come home.

I'd gone out the night before, swearing to Monica it was just for a few drinks. She started to challenge me on this, but I was out the door before the argument could gather any momentum. I didn't want to hear it. Before long, I was in Tampa, and soon after, drunk with friends in a club. I saw the dealer, my dealer. My guy.

"Doc, nice to see you," he said, which, of course, was his opening line in the pending business transaction. Dealers never, ever ask directly if you're interested in buying. That's too unprofessional and, besides, an easy way to get locked up, especially if the dude you're talking to happens to be an undercover cop.

Instead, it was left to me to open the dialogue. I told him, "Meet me down the street. Wait five minutes after I leave."

I was trying to be so nonchalant, thinking that if I didn't walk out the door with the dealer, no one would figure out that I was buying from him. That was my first mistake. I wasn't fooling anyone. The second mistake was buying too much, using too much, and getting so high, I thought I was going to die.

By now, everyone in the sports world knew what'd happened to Len Bias, the college basketball star who died of a cocaine overdose, just as he was about to start a career with the Celtics. His heart literally exploded from the strain of the drug. I'd heard about it, but never experienced it—until now. My heart was beating so fast, so hard, I didn't think my rib cage would be able to contain it. I'd been driving around, my usual routine, but I was too scared to even stay in my car. Instead, I pulled into the parking lot of a hotel, got out, checked in, and lay down on the bed.

Of course I should've gone home—I should've been home in the first place—but I didn't dare let Monica see me this out of control. I thought that if I could lie down, even for an hour, the drugs would pass through me and I could at least make a telephone call.

It was three in the morning. I thought that by four, I'd feel better, and by five or six, I could slip in the door, crawl into bed with Monica, and do my apologizing at breakfast. But my body wasn't on the same schedule. By four, I was still on the bed; I hadn't moved a muscle. Instead, I was sweating profusely, my heart still on some insane sprint to nowhere.

In fact, I realized that I couldn't move. Nothing. I was paralyzed—by fear, by adrenaline, by the power of the cocaine. And, maybe, by the early stages of death. I had never, ever experienced such terror in my life. Complete and utter paralysis. I was sinking fast, too far down to even open my mouth and scream for help.

I had visions of the ambulance crews bursting into the room. Tubes everywhere. Doctors, cops, clergymen, my family. I saw myself being lifted into an ambulance, into the emergency room, being administered CPR. I saw myself dying. I *was* dying.

So this is what it's like, I thought. You scream and scream on the inside, and no one hears you. You fall into a pit so black, you eventually give in and let the blackness swallow you up. You close your eyes and just go.

I don't know how long I remained on the bed, thinking I was going to die. It might've been an hour or three or four. I only know that, somehow, I eventually was able to move my arms and legs. I got up, went to the bathroom, and threw up until I almost passed out.

When I looked in the bathroom mirror, I saw a monster looking back at me. Drawn, haggard, utterly spaced-out and washed-out. I could only imagine what Monica and the kids would say if I walked into the house looking like this.

I wonder what the Mets would think, the millions of Met fans in New York and around the country. The great Doc, reduced to this. Well, one thing was for sure: there was no way I was going to show up at the party, not in this condition.

I didn't care how much grief I'd have to take from Monica, or how much of a bad memory this would leave with our children. Having their father stagger in the door, stinking of alcohol, and vomit, still sweating cocaine through his pores—*that* would be a debt I could never repay my children.

So I took the only possible route. I concocted a lie. I called Monica and said that I'd been in Orlando visiting some buddies from my minor-league days, but that on the way home the Mercedes had a flat. And because the wheels were custom-designed, the AAA guy couldn't repair the flat; they had to call for a special part.

It sounded plausible. I mean, I put a lot of money into my cars and bought special wheel covers. So I thought I could create enough doubt in Monica's head that . . . well, maybe I was telling the truth. No dice. She listened to me for a moment or two, then cut me right off.

"Dwight, why is it always me that's covering for you? Why do you make me lie for you?" she said, before hanging up.

I could hear the kids in the background. The party had started and Monica was already telling everyone that I was away on business. She was right: I was forcing her to lie to her family and friends, just to cover up my own sickness.

Monica didn't believe me for one second. She knew that I'd fallen, one more time. She knew that every time I called that afternoon, just to see if there were still people in the house, I was in hiding. I couldn't show up until every last person was gone, until it was safe for Doc Gooden, negligent father, to finally push the front door open and sneak into his bedroom without anyone seeing.

That would've been the easy way. But God wanted me to know just how badly I'd messed this one up. When I finally arrived home, late in the day, one or two steps from death, Ariel was there. Right there. And with this voice that couldn't have been any more loving or innocent, she said, "Daddy, where were you today?"

My lips started to form an answer, but no words came out. Instead, I just ran my hand over her beautiful face and asked the Lord to please give me strength, to help me find the path that would allow me to watch my children grow up. And then I went into my bedroom, lay down, and cried myself to sleep.

I HONESTLY DON'T know how long I would've kept spiraling downward like this, but obviously, Major League Baseball wasn't going to let me go unsupervised, or unpunished. I got a phone call in mid-September from Dr. Solomon. He told me, "The Executive Council is going to be meeting and talking about you." I had no doubt it was about the positive test results.

On September 15, in conjunction with MLB, the Mets announced to the world that I'd had another positive test—a tip-of-the-iceberg statement, since they said it was only one. There'd been others, but I guess the Mets didn't see the need to expose my downfall so openly to the world.

The bigger news, however, was Joe McIlvaine's pronouncement that I wouldn't be returning to Shea in 1995. Even though the strike still hadn't been settled, and I couldn't have been negotiating with the Mets anyway, the club nevertheless washed its hands of me. I'd embarrassed them one too many times, it seemed. I was totally and unconditionally on my own.

A part of me cursed the Mets for their heartlessness, but my more rational side knew none of this was the Mets' fault. In fact, I'd been half expecting them to cast me aside any day now. If Davey Johnson had still been the manager, maybe it would've been a different scenario. Certainly, if I'd pitched better, the Mets might've rationalized keeping me a little longer on the roster. But that was an era long gone, and if I was going to have another chance in baseball, it'd have to be with another team.

So the free fall continued, and in the ensuing days and weeks one of the ways I punished myself was by driving fast. Too, too fast. It was a way of covering up a growing depression, a realization that maybe I would never be able to stop using drugs. I'd failed several more tests in September and October 1994, and at one point MLB's doctors recommended that I start using Prozac.

I'd never heard of it before, but the doctors said it was for depression. There's no doubt I was feeling hopeless, but that was *after* I'd gotten high. I tried the Prozac, but I quickly learned that it couldn't do anything about the actual urges. It was essentially useless to me.

I took to the highways like a madman. I'd go to Tampa, have a few drinks with friends at our favorite clubs, and them—*bam*—I'd get high again. After that, I'd check into a hotel to let the coke have its way with me in private, and then, at dawn, I'd head home, beaten.

The thought that I'd lost another round pushed me down even further, made me even more desperate and depressed. It made me so damned angry that as I crossed the Howard Frankland Bridge, I'd push the Mercedes to 100 miles an hour . . . hell, I was just getting warmed up at those speeds.

One twenty, 130. I didn't care how fast I was going. The faster I went, the faster my heart raced, the more alive I felt, the better it felt. I was on the edge—far, far away from my core, which was feeling this awful pain.

At the outer regions of my sanity, I didn't care if I saw a cop. Hell, I *wanted* to be pulled over. I deserved it. I wanted to be arrested, handcuffed, taken to jail, tossed into some holding cell with the other animals. I *was* an animal, a drug user who was *out of control.*

I didn't deserve Monica's love or the adoration of my children. I didn't deserve the loyalty from my parents, or my friends' help. I didn't deserve to be a major league baseball player—not when I was getting high all the time.

Driving that fast was an act of desperation. I was either trying to commit suicide, or else crying out for help. I still don't know which. I was certain of this much, though: all I wanted was to push the Mercedes as fast as it would go. Once upon a time, when I was happier, I used to have fun speeding along in the Benz, when my friends and I used to take our cars along I-275 in St. Petersburg at nightfall for our own drag-racing contests.

We'd actually be bold enough to close off the entrance ramps along the way, setting up barricades so no cars could enter. We'd have an undisturbed stretch of highway that ran seven or eight miles. We'd get six or seven cars—Mercedes SL500s, BMW 850s, Buick Grand Nationals, Mustang GTs—and then let the engines take over the night. It wasn't uncommon for us to cross the finish line, near the south end of St. Pete, at speeds over 140 mph. It was a rush so intense, it became its own form of addiction.

The irony is that in all those races, all those nights when we commandeered I-275, we never saw a single cop. And the same was true again on those nights when I took to the highway by myself, looking for help. Not one state trooper on patrol. Not one speed trap. Not even a local cop sleeping in his cruiser.

It was just me and lonely road, driving so fast sometimes it felt like the asphalt would liquefy under my tires. I'd hold on to the steering wheel so tight, I thought I'd break the bones in my hands. I negotiated turns in half seconds, devoured miles as if they were feet. Occasionally I'd pass a car doing the speed limit, and if I didn't check my rearview mirror right away, he'd be gone before I finished blinking.

I did these things to give my guilt and my rage an outlet. With the rpm near five thousand, the engine of my Mercedes was loud enough to drown out my voice, which was at full volume, shouting: *Why can't I quit?*

I'd come home, crawl into bed, and say nothing to Monica, who, by now, had stopped asking questions. She knew where I'd been, but she no longer wanted to fight about it. I really couldn't blame her. Little by little that fall, Monica and the kids started to move on with their lives, leaving me alone in the cocoon of addiction.

Although there were many days when I was sober and drug-free, and remained indoors with my family without incident, my pattern was nevertheless set, and my family was learning to work around me.

I mean, there were instances when, by the time I'd get home in the morning, Monica would already be on her way out the door, taking the kids to school. If I knew we were going to cross paths like that, I'd deliberately wait in my car two blocks away, just so I wouldn't have to face any of them. It was that bad.

On November 4, however, after a night out with my friends and getting high, I managed to make it back to St. Pete by breakfast time. Which isn't to say that I sat down with everyone in the kitchen. Instead, I poured myself into the couch in the living room, careful not to let anyone get too close. I was still too high from the night before. When Monica and the kids left, I could only think: damn, too drugged up to even wish my kids a good day before school. How much worse does it get?

Maybe it was no surprise, then, that on that same day, the mailman came to my door to deliver a certified letter. It was from Bud Selig, and I knew it was bad news. The envelope was too thin, too stern looking, for it to be anything except punishment for my recklessness.

For a moment I considered not signing for the letter—just slamming the door in the postman's face and running upstairs. How could Selig hurt me if he couldn't get his message across? That thought lasted all of a second.

By now, I knew there was no running. Like all the other mistakes in my life, I knew that sooner or later I'd have to take responsibility for them. I signed, wished the mailman a nice day, and then sat on the couch to open the letter. I read it once, then put it down.

Were my eyes deceiving me?

I read the letter again. And again. And then a fourth time.

It was true: Selig had reached across the country and punched me squarely in the face. Knocked me right on my butt, as a matter of fact.

He wrote that because I'd failed so many tests, my suspension would extend through the entire 1995 season. There was a sentence or two about wishing me well, urging me to keep working hard, and his hope for my speedy return. And that was it.

I didn't move off the couch for almost an hour. I'm thankful no one was home, but they would've seen me looking like my life was over. I can't say I was surprised Selig took action against me, but I thought, at most, I'd get another thirty days tacked onto my suspension in 1995.

But a full year? What was I going to do? How was I possibly going to fill up the days of my life without baseball—and even worse, without any *hope* of baseball? I had no answers to these questions, which is why I told no one in the family about the letter. Not that night. Not until I'd gone out, bought a six-pack, driven to Tampa, and gotten as high as is humanly possible.

That was my answer to MLB's concern about me getting high—getting high again. One more peek into the blackness that had swallowed me up long ago. Somehow, at some point during the night, I'd reached my breaking point. By the time I came home the next day, I decided I couldn't fight the drugs anymore. I wouldn't.

This bout was *over,* and I was going to win, one way or another. If it couldn't be in a conventional way, through doctors and therapy and counseling, then I'd have to improvise. But one thing was for damned sure—I was not going to live the rest of my days on this earth as a drug addict, some junkie who sleeps in crackhouses and washes windshields for spare change.

I was sitting in my room, feeling the exhaustion of my failures. I was tired of lying to Monica, tired of seeing the hurt on my mother's face when she saw me sleeping the days away. Tired of my father's silence, which was a sure sign of his heartbreak.

I was tired of the newspaper headlines trumpeting my fall. Tired of hearing how my career was over, that I was a failure, a loser. And mostly, I was tired of feeling that urge—the beast that is always hungry, always craving more coke and laughing at my attempts to get clean and sober.

It was time to end this street fight, all right. I reached into my dresser and found the nine-millimeter automatic that I kept. I'd bought it for Monica to use as protection when I was away on road trips. She never liked to handle it, though, never even wanted to look at it. I doubt it'd even been touched since the last time I put it in the dresser, right under my pressed shirts.

The gun felt perfect in my hand; cool and sleek and perfectly weighted. Calmly, I loaded a full magazine, unlocked the safety, and placed the gun to my head. This was easier than I'd ever imagined it to be. All I had to do was squeeze the trigger, ever so slightly, and it would be done.

Would it hurt? Would I die instantly? Would I see my life flash before my eyes, just the way they say it does on TV? Suddenly I was full of questions. Would the sound of gunfire attract any attention?

Would my brains be splattered all over the walls?

Should I leave Monica a note?

I hadn't considered that, not until this very last moment. It was the only fair thing to do, I guess. My death—no, my *suicide*—would cause her unending pain and scar my children. The least I could do was tell them I was doing it for *them,* to release them from this sorry existence I'd forced them to be part of.

I put the gun on the bed and found a piece of paper. I sat at my desk and started to write two notes, one to my wife, the other to my children. I wanted to make it simple and honest, maybe just three words: I love you. Would that be enough to ease the horror of seeing me sprawled out on the floor, bleeding like that cat Kevin Mitchell had decapitated?

Maybe it would be better to call our voice mail and leave Monica a message, tell her I loved her over the phone. I picked up the phone and actually started to call our other number in the house, but changed my mind again, going back to Plan A, which was to just end it. Clean and quick, as merciless as possible.

I put the gun to my temple, then my ear, my forehead, then at the roof of my mouth. Hell, I couldn't even find clarity in suicide. What the hell was I doing? I must've killed off an hour that way, not wanting to live anymore, but not really wanting to die, either.

When the door handle finally turned, I think the barrel was right between my eyes. All I heard was a scream.

"Dwight, my God . . . no!" Monica shouted, sprinting across the room and wrestling me to the bed. She tried to pry the gun loose from my fingers, and God knows, I was glad she was there. But for some reason, I wouldn't let go. To do so would mean explaining all this. All of it: the drugs, the lifestyle I'd created, Selig's letter, and my attempt at suicide.

"Mon, just leave me alone," I said, already starting to cry.

"No, baby . . . just give me the gun," she said. Monica called for my mother, who must've walked in the house with her. She was in the bedroom in seconds. She and my wife managed to pry the gun free, and we sat there, all three of us hugging and crying. All I could think was: What have I done to be blessed by so much love?

# S E V E N

THERE COMES A point in everyone's life when the toughest decisions have to be made—and acted upon. After the gun incident, I knew if I didn't stop using, I would indeed eventually pull that trigger. I knew that unless I committed my entire world to sobriety, I was doomed, not just professionally but personally. I wouldn't last another year on this earth at the rate I was going.

So I quit baseball.

I called my agent, Jim Neader, and I called Gene Orza, the Players Association's associate counsel, telling them both I wanted to retire. Money wasn't a problem; I'd made enough to live on, and besides, I figured sooner or later I'd find something else to do with my time.

Neader, of course, was shocked. He'd been with me since my rookie year and had been a loyal friend, not just a businessman. Still, Jim knew I was having trouble and said if this was really my wish, then he'd do everything in his power to help me settle into a postbaseball life.

Orza was also supportive, although he suggested I wait until I'd officially completed the last 14 days of my suspension before retiring. And even then, Orza said, it was wiser not to file any papers severing my ties to the Major Leagues. As he put it, "You never know, you might want to change your mind someday. This way, you'll still be a free agent."

I held off on the paperwork, as Orza advised me to, but I still thought he was dead wrong. Between all the relapses, the three straight sub-.500 seasons, and the fact that I no longer had a team to call my own . . . well, surely there was something else for me out there. Maybe I could run youth camps in St. Petersburg, teaching kids to play while not making the same mistakes I did. I could open a restaurant or gymnasium. Or maybe I could coach. But pitching? Not anymore.

It was still early, a few weeks before Thanksgiving, when I was hanging outside my house with my nephew Gary Sheffield and a couple of guys we'd hired for private security. Someone had called my sister Betty on the phone earlier in the day and threatened to kill her—a mean-spirited prank, obviously, but serious enough for me to get some protection.

The block I lived on, a cul-de-sac, had only seven houses, five of which were owned by me and/or my nephew Gary. We each had one, my parents had another, and two of my sisters each had one, also. It was like our own private community, so we were naturally suspicious of any unfamiliar automobile traffic that came our way.

So there we were, watching the block, checking out the sunset, and generally killing time, when the conversation turned to my retirement. I could tell Gary had been meaning to talk to me about this for a few days now, as if the words were at the tip of his tongue. Now was his chance.

"So why you gonna retire, anyway?" Gary asked. His disappointment was obvious. For years, Gary had always dreamed of being my teammate, and now that he was playing for the Marlins and I was a free agent, it seemed like his wish could come true.

That is, until I retired. Gary, one the National League's best home-run hitters—best hitters, period—wasn't going to let me off very easily.

"You really tired of baseball, Doc? You don't like pitching anymore?" he said.

"It ain't that," I said. "I'm tired of everything. All the bullshit I been putting up with. You know what I'm saying?"

"Oh, I get it," Gary said, nodding. He got quiet for a moment. Finally, he blurted out what he'd been thinking all along.

"You mean you're afraid of the tests," he said.

"What?"

"They're too tough for you, aren't they? You can't beat those tests, so you're just walking away," he said, this time more forcefully. "You gonna let that shit end your career."

This time he just shook his head and walked away. I was so embarrassed at his accusation, I couldn't even muster a response.

Gary was right, of course. My retirement from baseball had nothing to do with the game itself. It was about the dreary routine of testing—positive result after positive result—that had driven me into the ground. I quit because I was too weak to fight. Too afraid to ask baseball for another chance. Too unsure that I could handle another reprieve.

I wanted to chase after Gary and tell him how right on target he was. How he opened my eyes with that one question. But just as I started to walk toward his house, a car I didn't recognize pulled up across the street. There were two guys inside and they stayed there, even after the headlights were cut.

My throat went dry immediately, thinking these were the people who'd promised to kill my sister. The three security guys I hired immediately fanned out toward the car, ready to handle the situation. I slid toward my car, ready to reach for the glove compartment, where I always kept a licensed pistol.

Just as things started to get tense, however, one of the men emerged from the car and identified himself. It was a New York sportswriter whom I'd know for years. I called off the bodyguards. Walking toward him, I said, "You almost got your ass kicked, you know that?"

We laughed at the near incident, before I was introduced to the other guy. His name was Ray Negron, a local guy who said he was friends with the writer and had merely given him a ride to my house.

I didn't say much to Negron; I regarded him as just another outsider looking for something, or trying to cash in on me, somehow. But he was polite, almost aggressively polite. He did most of the talking.

"I've been around baseball for almost twenty years," he said. "I played some minor-league ball, but I've been with the Yankees in every capacity you can think of. I was Reggie Jackson's right-hand man in the seventies. Right now I'm an agent, and I do some work for the Tokyo Giants, sending American ballplayers to Japan."

Negron said he was from Queens, and he bore a strong resemblance to John Candelaria, the tough lefty who hung around the big leagues for a long time in the eighties. Ray was 40, but looked younger. Mostly, he looked like a New Yorker, like he had some street smarts. But one thing I noticed was that he wasn't afraid to make eye contact with me, and I liked that. Ray gave me his card and told me he lived less than two miles away.

"Anytime you want to talk, you know where to find me," Ray said. We left it at that. That night, I wondered if he was serious about Japanese baseball. I knew it was a different style of baseball and a lot of Americans never made the transition because of the culture gap and the language barrier. But it was worth a shot. Hell, staring at a yearlong suspension, I would've gladly gone to Mars for a chance to pitch again.

But, obviously, I needed to take care of my drug problem first. I'd managed to find a temporary oasis of sobriety in the last week, and I wanted to keep it going. Maybe that's why I took Negron up on his offer to pay him a visit.

I brought my daughter Ariel with me, because Ray had said he had two kids around the same age. I knocked on his door and proceeded to spend the entire afternoon there. I knew right away that Negron understood the hell I was living in, because his first question wasn't about baseball, it was about drugs.

"You're thinking some days that it's hopeless, right?" Ray asked. I just nodded.

"I've been there, Doc," he said. "I lost a brother to drugs, my best friend fucked up a successful career on Wall Street because he loves crack, and me, I lost every penny I ever made because of my own gambling addiction.

"Dude, it was so bad that one day I was ripping the satellite dish off my fuckin' roof because I knew I could sell it for $500. I just *knew* that $500 was going to make me rich at Belmont—which of course it didn't. So don't ever let anyone look down at you because you've got a problem with coke. We all have problems; they just show up in different places."

No one had ever spoken to me that honestly, that directly. Negron never talked about baseball, even though the wall in his office was covered with pictures of Reggie Jackson and Billy Martin. There were clipped articles about the Yankees, framed back pages of the New York *Post* and *New York Daily News,* back from the seventies.

Negron had been the Yankees' batboy, their video specialist, and had worked one-on-one with Reggie. He wasn't some con man. The pictures on the wall backed him up.

"Someday you can be on that wall, too, Doc," Negron said. "But first you have to get your life together."

He told me that if I was really serious about getting help, he could put me in touch with people in the St. Pete area. Ray said, "It isn't going to be the pretty stuff, like Betty Ford. But it'll open your eyes, dude."

I told him, yes, I wanted help. And that's how I ended up with my first real-life sponsor, Ray's buddy Vincent Kenyon, who was trying to fight his own drug habit.

Vincent, forty-three, was from New York, like Ray, although he was on a much faster track to success than Negron ever was. Harvard-educated and working for a top Wall Street firm in the early nineties, Vincent's first fall came when he was about to close a major deal that would've netted him several hundred thousand dollars.

He went to a party on Friday, tried a little coke, and didn't come home for four days. He missed the closing of his deal and soon after lost his job. Ever since, for the last three years, Vincent's pattern would be to slowly rebuild his career, work toward a financial coup—and then relapse just as he was about to make his money. Even worse, he was battling not just coke, but crack.

"Doc, if you ever think of cocaine as a mellow high, like slowly climbing stairs, then using crack is like taking an express elevator all the way to the top," Vincent said. "It's a very powerful high and in many people it creates paranoia. You think everyone is out to get you, you think everyone is an undercover cop. You cannot defeat crack unless you get help. If you're in denial, it will kill you."

That was the type of counseling I was getting now; from real people who told real stories about their own addictions. When I went to my first counseling meeting with Vincent and Ray, I wasn't surrounded by wealthy businessmen and members of the social elite, like at Betty Ford. This was a collection of twenty or so addicts from the street, gathered in a run-down section of town. And the man who ran the meeting was as raw and unpolished as anyone I'd ever met.

His name was Ron Dock, and as I came to learn, he was a forty-five-year-old Bronx native and a former marine who'd served in Vietnam. Dock stood six feet, and he couldn't have been more than 160 pounds, but he still had muscles in that thin, wiry sort of way.

I sat in the corner of the converted living room, and I was deeply impressed by how simple and unpretentious the meeting was. Each addict stood up before the group and told his story. Some relived their initial fall into drugs, others talked about their most recent urges and dark days, others simply came to celebrate one more day of sobriety.

I learned that the actual words that were spoken were less important than the act of sharing. It's important for an addict to know he's not alone. Hence the idea of one-on-one sponsorship. Right away I knew I was ready for twelve-step recovery, the foundation upon which Narcotics Anonymous is built.

Still, I was totally blown away when Dock took his turn in front of the group. He told a story I will never forget.

"I went to Evander Childs High School in the Bronx, and I was going nowhere in my life," Dock said. "I was boxing in the PAL, running a little track, but I had no real goals. I didn't know anything about the marines or Vietnam until one of my buddies, an older guy, came home one day in his dress blues. And, man, he wiped me off the map. He looked so tough, so sharp. I was bored with my life at the time: I decided I had to join up.

"Funny thing was, I didn't know the first thing about racism until I got into the corps. The sergeants started telling me, 'Hey, boy, we're gonna kill you when we get you to 'Nam. You gonna die, you know that?' Shit, I thought these guys were supposed to be on my side. Was I scared? You better believe it. I was only seventeen when I went over, and I got into my first firefight within two weeks.

"It was three in the afternoon, and I was part of a seven-man patrol getting ready to set up an ambush when we got caught in an L-shaped ambush ourselves. The VC started with mortars, then with AK-47 fire, and right away we were pinned down in the rice paddies. We lost one Marine and another was about two minutes away from dying when we called in for an auxiliary strike. Luckily, the VC broke off contact with us.

"Well, it happened so fast, I never realized that during the firefight I had urinated and defecated on myself. I was screaming, completely crazy; I'd gone into shock. I knew Vietnam wasn't for me, but there I was, stuck in the worst place in the world. My buddy in the dress blues didn't tell me what being a marine was really about—constant fear. And, man, I was about over the edge. My sergeant gave me a little weed, some Jim Beam, and I passed out. And that's how it started."

I was fascinated by this man and how raw his world was. I thought I had it bad? Dock said he got high every single night in Vietnam, particularly when he was on night patrol. "Put it this way," Dock said. "Whenever we killed a VC, we checked his pockets for opium."

The irony is that Dock's addiction went beyond weed; he was hooked on fear itself, so much so, that he eventually began volunteering for night patrol. No wonder he came back to the U.S. totally out of control. He took over a Veterans Administration hospital one day, holding doctors and patients alike as hostages until the cops could subdue him.

Not surprisingly, Dock was dishonorably discharged from the marines, which only accelerated his downward spiral. In the coming years, he said, "I was in jail, psychiatric wards, and mostly in the street. Then one day it came to me, man. I was eating out of a garbage bin here in St. Pete, down to 140 pounds, and I thought to myself, 'This is the day I'm going to die.'

"So I went up to a cop and said, 'Please, take me to a treatment center.' That's how I ended up here, and I've been sober for three years now."

Dock must've spoken for a half hour nonstop, and even though the other people in the room must've heard this story before, it was obvious they absorbed its message. I did, too. When the meeting ended I walked up to Dock and said I could relate to everything he'd said.

I expected Ron to smile and welcome me aboard. The people at Betty Ford and Smithers had been so friendly and supportive, why wouldn't he be as well?

Instead, Dock looked me right in the eye and said, "How bad do you want to stay clean?"

"Real bad," I answered.

"If you do, then just come back here tomorrow," Dock said. "Don't say another word. You're talking too much as it is. The only way you can prove you're serious is if you show up tomorrow."

Just that simply, something changed in my life. With Vincent as my partner, Ray as my professional attachment, and guided by Ron Dock—this crazy, skinny ex-marine who couldn't have cared less that I was a professional athlete—I was ready to venture into a brave, new world of sobriety.

EVERY DAY, RON Dock preached the same lesson, until it became cemented in my head: change the people, places, and things that feed your addiction. Change your surroundings, stay away from bars, cut off old friends, your enablers. Turn your back on them, even if it breaks your heart.

I was put to that test late in 1994, when an old buddy of mine was in trouble. His name was Troy: years earlier, he had been my best friend. We grew up in the same neighborhood, played ball together, got into the usual mischief. But even back then there was a strange anger about him. Troy always wanted to fight other kids from the neighborhood. Even though he never turned that temper on me, I was always a little scared of him.

Troy ended up becoming a professional boxer—a small career, nothing that ever got off the ground. Still, he was good at what he did, when he was able to stay in the ring. Troy was having domestic problems with his girlfriend, Angela. It was his temper that ruined his relationship.

Troy could be a jealous guy, and one time during an argument that fall, he beat the girl up pretty badly. She got a restraining order, but three weeks later Troy lost his temper again and this time threw his woman through a windshield.

It was a bad day for everyone. Angela's face was so badly cut, she needed a skin graft from her hip. And of course Troy ended up in jail. This time he was in serious trouble with the law. The prosecutor wanted to send him away for two to three years.

I went to visit Troy in the Hillsborough County Jail and the first thing he told me was he couldn't do the time.

"Doc, I ain't going to no jail."

I was stunned.

"What are you talking about, man? You're here. They got you."

"I'd rather die than end up there, cuz. Look, I got a plan."

Troy told me about an escape route he believed could spring him. He'd been thinking about it for days, and really believed it was foolproof. But he would need my help.

First, Troy planned on causing such a commotion in the courtroom before sentencing that the judge would have no choice but to order a bailiff to remove him.

Troy knew there was a back room where disorderly prisoners were kept—I suppose he'd spent that much time in courtrooms—and it was guarded by just one bailiff. That's where Troy thought I could help.

"Soon as they take me back there, I'm gonna tell my lawyer to get you. I'm gonna tell him I need to talk to you," he said. "You get back there, and then I want you to distract the guard. Talk to him about baseball, or anything. But call him outside the little room and get his attention."

"And?"

"And then? I'm busting out," Troy said. "The exit is two floors down. I know exactly how to get out of that place."

"What about your handcuffs?" I asked.

"No sweat, cuz. I know how to get out of 'em. Whaddaya say, man, you gonna help me?"

I was speechless.

"Come on, man. This is gonna be my shot. My only shot. You gotta help me, Doc. I ain't doin' no jail time, that's for damn sure."

It must've been a full minute before I answered. Finally, I said, "We'll see, Troy."

"We'll see? That mean you gonna be in court?"

"Yeah," I said, still not sure which direction I was going. "I'll be there."

His eyes lit up.

"My man!"

His sentencing was scheduled for ten days after that visit, and right until the moment I entered the courtroom, I was undecided. I would wake up at night, thinking of my buddy depending on me like that, and the obligation I felt to him. But I also knew, in my heart, Troy was crazy.

Any doubt about his state of mind was wiped out when I entered the courthouse. The place was full of cops, and every exit had its own special guards. What was Troy thinking of? How could I have been so weak not to say no right on the spot?

I saw Troy being led into the room with a bunch of other prisoners, and I have to admit, I was shocked at what a criminal he looked like. He was wearing a bright orange jumpsuit, handcuffed, being watched by a huge cop who looked like he was waiting for an excuse to beat the shit out of him.

I was in the general-seating area, as if I was watching a movie I'd already seen. Just as Troy promised, he started a commotion in the courtroom.

"This shit is a frame-up, man. Y'all setting me up," he shouted.

The judge, an elderly woman, reacted immediately.

"The prisoner will keep quiet, or I'll have him removed immediately."

And that was just what Troy was waiting to hear.

"Yeah, that's right . . . remove my ass. Throw away the fuckin' key. Y'all a bunch of racist motherfuckers, anyway. Don't matter if I'm here or not, I'm guilty. Ain't that right, Your Honor?"

By now, Troy was fidgeting in his chair, bouncing around like he was on crack. If I hadn't known better, I would've actually thought he was high at that moment. The judge, already in a bad mood, sure didn't need any more provocation. Being called a racist was all she needed to hear in order to throw Troy right out.

"Bailiff, remove the prisoner . . . *now*," she thundered.

And just like Troy predicted, he was led away, screaming like a crazy person. Suddenly I was the one sweating. I had to make a choice . . . *now*. Almost instantly, Troy's lawyer tapped me on the shoulder.

"Mr. Gooden, Troy would like to speak to you for a moment," the attorney whispered in my ear. "He's in a holding area in the back."

Troy was there, all right. The lawyer left me at the door of a little cell and excused himself, saying he had to return to the courtroom. And just like Troy predicted, there was one guard. He was friendlier than I expected.

"Hey, you're Dwight Gooden! The ballplayer! I'm a big Mets fan," the guard said, smiling. He let me in to talk to Troy, then went back to his post at the door.

Troy's eyes were on fire—that's how charged up he was, believing his scheme was working.

"Man, I told you I could get out of here," Troy said, whispering. "The fucking guard even *likes* you. So go ahead, cuz, go outside, talk to him about some baseball shit."

I looked at Troy, not knowing what to say. His scheme was so hopeless. There was no way we'd ever get out of that courthouse alive. There was no way I could help him without getting into deep trouble myself. That's all I needed now that I was trying to remain sober—getting arrested for helping a prisoner escape from a courthouse. I was finally at the crossroads. I was out of time.

"Guard, can I talk to you a minute?" I said to the cop.

Troy's eyes were almost popping out of his head. He was ready to bolt.

I stepped over toward the cop. I could see Troy poised in his chair, almost in a football-like crouch. Any second now, and he'd be gone. All the guard had to do was turn his back.

"Do me a favor," I said. My heart thundered out of control. I could've sworn the cop heard it.

"Sure, Doc," he said. "What is it?"

I took one final deep breath.

"Make sure no one hurts Troy," I said as I turned and walked out the exit, leaving Troy in the holding cell.

"Doc . . . *Doc*," I heard Troy yelling after me, the panic in his voice breaking me up inside. But I kept walking. As I reached the door, I heard Troy start to cry. By now, I was running, hoping I was far enough away that Troy couldn't hear me sobbing, too.

I don't remember ever feeling as low as I did the rest of that day. For Troy. For myself. For my own life that I was trying to piece together. As desperate as Troy was—and he did end up going to jail for 18 months—I knew that just a few months earlier, that could've been me.

# EIGHT

BY EARLY 1995, I had narrowed my world to two key goals: staying drug-free—which meant going to group counseling every single day—and trying to get back to baseball. My hopes of pitching in Japan were dashed after Ray did a little investigating. He found out that my two drug-related suspensions had scared off the Japanese, which I can't say surprised me. If the Mets wouldn't take another chance on me, even after all the good years I'd given them, why would a group of strangers?

Instead, I decided to focus on working myself into shape, with the hope of an early reinstatement. If I could prove to the Executive Council that I was taking my recovery seriously—producing a string of negative tests, throwing and running diligently, plus working in the community, especially with kids—then who knows, maybe I could pull off a small miracle.

Through Ray, I met a New York attorney named Bill Goodstein, who'd represented Dave Righetti in the eighties and still had a good relationship with George Steinbrenner. Goodstein was also friendly with White Sox owner Jerry Reinsdorf, who happened to be serving on the Executive Council. I felt Goodstein offered me the best chance at reinstatement, and as much as it hurt me to make the switch, I told Jim Neader that Goodstein would be representing me in the coming season.

So that spring, while Goodstein and Ray worked the phones and wrote letters on my behalf, I began a simple but unrelenting workout routine, designed to help me reclaim my pitching skills. Every morning Ray, Vincent, and I would head over to nearby Eckerd College, where I'd would throw and run, then lift weights in the gym.

Talk about a comedown: after years of playing on perfectly manicured fields in the big leagues, I was reduced to the barely cut grass at Eckerd, pitching in my shorts and a cut-up T-shirt, and throwing to Ray and Vincent, neither of whom was really qualified to catch me.

Still, it was a reminder of how far I'd fallen and that it was no one's fault but my own. At least I had professional help in the conditioning aspect. I hired Larry Mayol, who used to be the Mets' trainer in the early eighties, and had since relocated to St. Petersburg, where he'd become a personal trainer.

Larry had me running and lifting four to five times a week. I was at the school by eight A.M. every single day, thanks to Ray, who kept me right on schedule. After the workouts, I'd drive to the health clinic for my drug test and then we'd go get lunch. In the afternoons, I'd help out coaching my son's Little League team, which, as I came to learn, gave me more pleasure than anything else I'd ever done in this life.

All this structure gave me a certain peace I hadn't experienced in years. In fact, my addiction went into a dormancy that both thrilled me and scared the hell out of me. How would I know if I was about to relapse?

Ron Dock had warned me, "Just because you're clean for five or six months doesn't mean you can't fall down tomorrow." He was absolutely right: I went seven years without using, from 1987 to 1994, and I never saw it coming.

All I could do was bury myself in this new universe. Besides coaching Little League, I hosted a once-a-week radio show in Tampa—another project that Ray hatched for me. His roommate, Doug Kemp, worked in the station's publicity department, and when they came to me with the idea of being on the air, it took me all of one second to agree.

It was good exposure for me—hell, it couldn't hurt to show the Executive Council that I was so reformed, I'd even become a member of the media. And, in the long run, doing interviews would teach me how tough a reporter's job can be.

Too many players dismiss journalists as mudslingers and troublemakers. A small percentage are, but a majority of the reporters I dealt with in New York—guys like John Giannone and Frank Isola and Mike Lupica from the *Daily News*, Danny Castellano from the Newark *Star-Ledger*, and Jack Curry from *The New York Times*, were fair-minded and honest.

In fact, I think every ballplayer should, at some point in his career, conduct a live, five-minute interview. Then they'd see that asking questions isn't so easy. In fact, it's like a conversation that you're responsible for keeping alive. I never realized until I was on the other side of the microphone that it was up to me to ask follow-up questions, being one step ahead of the player I was interviewing.

That's why I always try to give reporters meaningful answers to their questions, because I know they need something to follow up with. Once I got the hang of it, the summer on the air was terrific fun. My guests included Darryl Strawberry, Pete Schourek, Fred McGriff, Reds general manager Jim Bowden, Seattle manager Lou Piniella, who's from Tampa, Yankee super scout Gene Michael, and Rangers' president Tom Grieve.

I had a really good time at Piniella's expense one day. I was in the studio in Tampa, and I knew the Mariners were in New York playing the Yankees. So I called the Stadium and had the operator put me through to the visiting manager's office.

Lou picked up the phone right away and said hello.

"Lou, it's Doc," I said. "Doc Gooden. How're ya doing?"

"Fine . . . great . . . hey, it's great to hear your voice," he stammered. I could tell that Lou thought I was nuts, calling him out of the blue like that. But I wasn't finished.

"Lou, look, I'm outside the Stadium right now and I need ten tickets," I said. "No, make it a dozen. Can you do that for me?"

Mind you, the Yankees and Mariners had created a fierce rivalry in 1995, and the Stadium was already sold out. Which is why Lou went from being puzzled to all-out panic in just one sentence.

"A *dozen*?" he said, his voice rising by an octave. "Well . . . okay, I guess. Just give me ten minutes and call me back."

By now I was laughing too hard to fool Piniella any longer. I told him I was in Tampa hosting my radio show, and I was actually calling to see if he'd be my guest.

Lou let out a long sigh and said, "Of course, Doc. Anything except twelve fucking tickets today."

IT WAS TURNING out to be a good spring and summer, although I'd be lying if I said it was a perfect one. All during the time I was working out and staying clean, I'd noticed unusual and troubling behavior from Vincent.

There'd be times I'd stop over at Ray's house and Vincent would be dead asleep on the couch in the living room. Actually, he'd be closer to unconscious. I'd try to wake him, but he'd barely open his eyes and say, "Man, I'm dead tired, lemme sleep."

I didn't think anything of it the first time, but when it started happening on a regular basis, it occurred to me that Vincent was using again. I was to learn later that he was sleeping off a crack high. That was the beginning, and things only got worse.

Another warning sign that I should've considered was that Vincent was close to finishing a deal to market prepaid calling cards. It was supposed to land him a good chunk of money, which I knew he needed. Vincent had been living off Ray, and was more or less penniless.

But this was supposed to be Vincent's breakthrough deal—enough to get him back on his feet, pay his debts, reemerge on Wall Street as the guy who'd been to hell and back. Until that point he had been just as committed as me to his sobriety, getting up every morning to run, attending NA meetings, and then staying at home once the sun went down.

But that all changed the night I got a phone call from Ray. The news was really, really bad. Vince had just gone down hard somewhere in St. Pete. He'd called Ray and said that he was being held hostage by a group of drug dealers.

Ray said, "I didn't want to bother you with this . . . Christ, Vincent's relapsed so many fucking times I've lost count."

I reminded Ray that all of us—me, him, Vincent, and Ron Dock—had made a promise to be there for each other. If one of us stumbled, all of us had vowed to act as the safety net. So how could I turn my back on Vincent now?

The real problem, though, was that Vincent was around Thirty-fourth Street, a bad part of town, and who knew how serious his emergency was? Ray said Vincent had already been missing for three days; he just disappeared after taking a group of investors to the airport. There it was: the success syndrome, knocking Vincent to the ground one more time.

No doubt, he'd gone on a crack binge and had run out of money by the third day. Now he needed cash to pay the dealers and the only one he could turn to was Ray, his lifelong buddy.

"Doc, I'm going to handle this myself," Ray said. "There's no need for you to be exposed to this. I just wanted you to know what's going on, in case something happens to me."

"Ray, I'm coming," I said. "You don't know your way around that neighborhood. You might end up getting shot."

"Yeah, and so could you," he said.

"Let me worry about that. I'll pick you up in five minutes."

When I got to Ray's house, Ron Dock was already there. The three of us decided to drive in Ray's beat-up Subaru, since my Mercedes would make us moving targets in a crack neighborhood. Before getting in the car, I decided to stuff five fifty-dollar bills in my pocket, figuring that sooner or later this would come down to paying for Vincent's life. I thought about bringing my gun, too, but I didn't want to push my luck.

When we reached Thirty-fourth Street, I discovered right away how bad the situation was. We found Vincent and three very dangerous-looking guys near a back alley. Ray told me, "Stay right here," because he obviously thought this crisis was going to get even uglier. "You're the one with a career to protect, not me," he said.

Ray and Ron went to appraise the situation, leaving me in the car. They were back moments later, looking fully panicked.

"Vincent's in some deep shit," Ray said. "These guys want money, and I don't think we should be fucking with them. Let's just give them what they want and get Vincent out of here."

"That's fine," I said, "but I want to talk to them first."

"Doc, what are you, nuts?" Ray said. "Let's just go."

"Not until I see what's happening," I said.

Ray saw there was no arguing with me, so the three of us walked up the alley. He was right: it *was* bad. The three guys, young and from the streets, were definitely pissed. One of them must've stood six four, over 250 pounds, all muscle. He had this hard, violent look to him. He was also holding a pistol at his side. I made sure to avoid eye contact with him, because, frankly, he scared the hell out of me.

Instead, I focused on Vincent, who hardly looked human anymore. He was wearing a business suit—obviously the same clothes he'd had on for three days—although he was curiously missing his socks and his shoes. The body odor was overpowering, like no stench I'd ever inhaled. He was lying in a pile of garbage, crying.

"I fucked up, man, I'm sorry," he said. "I'm sorry, Doc."

The hard-looking guy kicked Vincent and said, "Shut the fuck up, motherfucker."

"What's the problem here?" I asked.

The dude turned his gaze on me, and for the first time I met it straight on.

"You gonna make me repeat myself?" he said. "This piece of shit owes us money. I ought to blow him away because he ain't worth all this trouble."

I don't why I decided to make a stand on Vincent's behalf. This situation wasn't worth risking my life, but I didn't like the guy's tone or his disrespect—for Vincent or for me. It was one thing to be owed money, but he was just humiliating Vincent for the sheer fun of it. So I decided to come to his defense.

"You got a relative of mine right there," I said, nodding in Vincent's direction. "I want him back."

I paused for effect, and then said, "Don't fuck with me, 'cause I'm strapped, too."

I knew I had just told two lies: I was neither related to Vincent, nor did I have a gun. I just prayed no one called my bluff. Out of the corner of my eye, I saw that Ray had gone so pale, it looked like he was close to having a heart attack.

This was a standoff, all right. I don't know what would've happened had the third dealer—seemingly the youngest—not broken the silence.

"Yo, man, you're Doc Gooden," he said. "I know you. What are you doing with this piece of shit?"

Sensing I was gaining the upper hand, I pushed the advantage.

"You call my cousin a piece of shit?" I said angrily. "To my face?"

"We got no beef with you, Doc. We know you're from the neighborhood," he said. "We just want our money. Motherfucker's been using what he can't pay for."

The big dude then leaned over and slapped Vincent on the back of the head and said, "Ain't that right, motherfucker?"

I decided I'd made my point, and Vincent had suffered enough. I pulled out the fifty-dollar bills and gave them to the big guy. He stared at the money, then stared at me. I wondered if this was going to turn into a holdup. If he demanded more, and pointed the gun on me, what could I have done? Apparently, though, the fact that his partner knew me defused the situation, because he put the money in his pocket and broke eye contact. We helped Vincent back to his feet, and when we were walking away, one of the dealers said to him, "Don't *ever* come back here."

I heard the big guy mumble, "We should've just shot the motherfucker."

We got into Ray's car, where, for the first time, I realized how scared I was. In fact, my hands were shaking. Vincent made a noise that sounded like a sob. Ron said to him, "We're taking you to a place where you can get help. You have to go. Your life depends on it. Next time you could end up dead."

Vincent started to protest, saying, "All I need is some food and some sleep," but I cut him off.

"If you don't go," I said, "then everything you've been telling me about recovery these last few months was bullshit. If you can't admit you're sick, how do you expect me to do it?"

"Surrender to it, man," Dock said. "Remember, if Custer had surrendered, he would've lived a long, long time. You're gonna die if you don't surrender."

Ray was already driving to a place called Prosperity Villa. Suddenly everyone became very quiet as Vincent stopped resisting. When we arrived, I put my arm around him and said, "We're here."

He didn't answer. Instead, I only felt the shaking of Vincent's shoulders as he cried.

## MAY 14, 1996 (CONTINUED)

FOR FIVE INNINGS, I operated on automatic pilot. By that I mean, I took the mound after every third out we made, I took the signs from Girardi, I made the best pitches that I could. I had no idea that I hadn't allowed a hit, or even that we were winning, 2–0. It sounds strange, but the deeper I got into the night, the further away I drifted.

Normally, I sit on the bench during our at-bats, because I like to see guys like Tino Martinez and Paul O'Neill hit. Plus, I can always get a sense of the opposing hitters' states of mind, based on how their pitcher is faring. If he's getting lit, there's a natural dampening effect on the offense. There's no comparison between facing a lineup that's down by a run, and one that's looking at a six-or seven-run deficit.

But on this night, I didn't spend much time on the bench, and I sure wasn't talking to anyone. Instead I walked a few steps up the runway between the dugout and the clubhouse—just a narrow catwalk that gave me the privacy I wanted.

A couple of guys saw me—the runway is in full view of anyone at the bat rack, or anyone on his way to the bathroom. But no one came over, which was probably the right thing to do. Once, after the sixth inning, I started crying, over nothing and everything.

The crowd had just given me a standing ovation after the top of the sixth and until then I just assumed all that energy from the stands came from the intense rivalry the Yankees had with the Mariners. After all, this was the first time Seattle had been in town since the '95 play-offs, and after the Yankees had taken the first two games of that series at home, it was still a terrible blow to all of New York that Seattle took the next three in the Kingdome.

So here they were, the big, bad Mariners, managed by Lou Piniella, the man Yankee fans both loved and hated. Loved him, because he was an integral part of the Yankee teams that were so dominant in the late seventies—especially that legendary '78 team. And hated him, because he was now an ex-Yankee, and had broken his former team's heart by leading the Mariners into the League Championship Series.

That's why I thought the crowd was so pumped. It was them, the Mariners, not me. I was in a daze, leaning against the wall in that runway, tears flowing down my cheeks.

"Doc, you okay?"

It was Steve Donahue, the Yankees' assistant trainer. He saw me there alone, and decided to offer a few words of advice, since his father had once undergone a similar open-heart surgery.

"Trying," I said, trying to compose myself.

"Think of your dad," Donahue said.

"Oh, I am, man," I said. "I can't stop worrying about him. You know how it is."

"What I'm saying is, think about him out there," Donahue answered. "Bring him out to the mound with you. Do it for him."

Donahue patted me on the chest and let me digest that thought. It made sense. My father had taught me everything I knew about baseball, so if there was ever going to be a time to draw on his strength and his love, it was now. The noise from the stands was getting louder now, as we'd just made the third out in the bottom of the sixth. Kenny Rogers came up the runway, handed me my glove, and said, "It's all yours, baby. Go get 'em."

When I stepped onto the field for the top of the seventh, I felt this surge from the crowd. And even though I'd never been a very spiritual person, at least not until I finally quit using drugs, I could've sworn I heard my father's voice in my head.

*Lift your leg. Stay on top of the ball. Follow through. Challenge the hitter.*

The funny thing is, for all the great years I had at Shea, I never did throw a no-hitter. Even with a fastball that sometimes got close to ninety-six mph and a curveball that was bigger and meaner than it is now, going nine innings without a hit was an accomplishment that had eluded me.

Maybe it wasn't supposed to happen to me back then. It would've been too easy, like everything else that came my way in the eighties. I would've taken a no-hitter for granted, assumed it was just another milestone coming to me. The way I so casually accepted the Rookie of the Year award and the Cy Young. And the way I missed the Mets' victory parade after we won the World Series in 1986. Those were mistakes I made from pride, from arrogance, from not understanding the gifts I'd been blessed with. In a way, I'm thankful I didn't throw that no-hitter as a Met, because I probably would've lost the memory of it in a haze of drugs and alcohol.

Now it was real to me. It was happening, and every single pitch became a miniature apocalypse. Any pitcher who tells you he enjoys throwing a no-hitter—at least while it's happening—is lying, because it's the most nerve-racking experience he's ever known.

By the time I took the mound in the ninth inning, the crowd created this sound, so loud it seemed to fill up the ballpark. No one was talking to me now—not Donahue, not Rogers, not Torre or Mel. Derek Jeter and Wade Boggs wouldn't even look at me as they ran out to short and third. It was just me and my dad's spirit, three outs away from making history.

Oh, that ninth inning made me sweat. It was terror, actually. I started it by walking Rodriguez even after I had him 1–2. All night, I kept that good, live fastball, but I sabotaged myself by overthrowing it, trying to blow it right by him. And I paid for it by throwing three heaters that weren't even close to being strikes.

I flashed a quick glance into the dugout, and I saw Mel on the phone to the bullpen. Of course. It made all the sense in the world. This was my no-hitter in progress, but it was also a close game, and regardless of whether I was able to chisel a place in the history books, the Yankees still wanted to win this one.

Griffey was due up next, which explained the growing concern in the dugout. Any American League pitcher will tell you how much damage Junior can do in one swing. He stands there, wiggling his bat in that defiant way of his, daring you to throw a fastball by him.

When he's right, which is about 99 percent of the time, Griff has one of the quickest bats in the league, and he generates incredible power with that slightly uppercut hack of his.

The only way to pitch Griffey is carefully, and just hope he'll chase something out of the strike zone. If you make a mistake, he'll kill you. I saw this for myself on television the previous October, when he took Coney deep in the eighth inning of Game Five of the division series. The Yankees had a 4–2 lead, and all Cone needed was six more outs, and they were headed for the League Championship Series.

But David never made it out of the inning, primarily because Griffey crushed a long home run to right, jumping all over a fastball. That was the beginning of the end of the Yankees in that series, as Cone eventually walked Doug Strange with the bases loaded, forcing the game into extra innings and an eventual 6–5 Yankee loss in the eleventh.

I was totally aware of that threat, which is why I pitched Griffey like the game depended on it. It did. One mistake, and not only would I lose this no-hitter, but the lead would vanish with it, too. I was locked in, focused, almost hypnotized by the mission before me. I threw a 1–1 curveball that broke mean and late—the seams spinning tight enough that it actually looked more like a slider to Griffey.

He swung, just a fraction of a second out in front, since I knew he'd be looking for another fastball. Instead, Griffey bounced to Tino Martinez's right. About two steps. I watched Tino field the ball. And then I froze.

Why? I still wonder, to this day. I watched in horror as Griffey turned into a blur running up the first-base line. I watched as Tino looked for me to cover the bag, and I wasn't there.

Run, I told myself.

Run.

Get there.

Now.

I was paralyzed, helpless as I sabotaged my own no-hitter. The race to the bag was between Tino and Griffey, and if my guy lost, my no-hitter was over. Martinez realized this, because I saw him do something no first baseman had ever tried.

With the ball in his glove, and sensing he no longer had time to actually run to touch the base, Tino dived headfirst, glove-first, in full desperation.

Incredibly, Martinez beat Griffey—thinking so quickly that he covered up for my lapse. The crowd went crazy, and in my head, I was cheering, too. But my heart was beating so fast, I couldn't even utter a word of thanks. Instead, I just took the ball from Martinez, who said simply, "Come on, Doc. Go get 'em."

My no-hitter was intact, and so was the 2–0 lead, for now. Rodriguez had taken second on the play, and I was faced with another emergency at the plate, Edgar Martinez, the defending

American League batting champion. He was the complete opposite of Griffey, but just as capable of wounding me.

Edgar has a "quiet" bat, with hardly any weight shift, and he very rarely chases a ball out of the strike zone. But he will attack quickly, silently, at the last moment, after letting you think you've beaten him with your best fastball.

I factored all this data into my head, took a deep breath, and committed yet another cardinal mistake: I overthrew the ball, thinking I had to exceed a hundred mph to beat Martinez. The result was a five-pitch walk that put runners on first and second, and when I threw a first-pitch fastball to Jay Buhner that bounced by Girardi, both runners advanced. I was closer than ever to being taken out of a game in which I hadn't surrendered a hit.

I knew this because I looked into the dugout, and this time Mel wasn't on the phone. He was already on the top step of the dugout, on his way out to the mound. I took some comfort in seeing that Torre wasn't the one visiting. If it'd been him, I was finished. But Mel's presence meant I had a chance to talk my way into at least another batter.

Mel is one of the most decent, honest coaches I've ever known. It's hard to explain, but there's something about his demeanor—so trusting, so trustworthy—that makes you want to tell him the truth. Not all pitchers lie to their coaches . . . well, yes, they do. Invariably, when a pitcher is asked in the late innings how he feels, especially with runners on base, any true competitor will say simply, "I feel fine."

Maybe that's why Mel didn't ask. He announced that he was on the mound to let me collect my thoughts.

"I'm not taking you out, Doc. I'm just here to give you a breather," Mel said.

He looked me straight in the eye, then looked at Girardi. Stottlemyre was waiting for either one of us to volunteer information. I knew I wasn't saying a word, unless asked.

Finally, Mel said, "This game is yours, Doc. Yours unless you tell me you can't go anymore."

That was all I needed to hear.

"I gotta have this guy," I said, referring to Buhner.

Stottlemyre waited a moment to let my announcement sink in. I guess I sounded convincing, because the next thing he said was, "Go get him."

The crowd roared in approval when Stottlemyre walked off the mound alone. They wanted to see history made, and truth was, so did I. My obstacle? Obviously, I needed to retire Buhner—no more walks, no more wild pitches—but I needed more than just an out. I needed a strikeout.

If only this was 1985, when all I had to do was begin that massive leg kick, throw the ball as hard as I could down the middle of the plate, and watch another hitter go down on strikes. It was so easy back then. But now, in 1996, in the ninth inning and after 120 pitches, I knew I'd have work hard to summon up the old heat.

Buhner was like so many other Mariners—a very aggressive, very strong hitter who was looking to do his damage against fastballs. My only hope was to bust him, up and in, and hope that his big swing would be a half second slower than my fastball.

So for the first time all night, I pretended it was '85 again. I threw the ball as hard as I could, with as much arm speed as my body would allow. One more time, I loaded up my rifle and hunted for a strikeout. I remember that, with the count at 1–0, after that wild pitch, I got a fastball over the inside corner that Buhner took for strike one.

Then I threw the fastball that I wanted, up and in, but it was too high, which ran the count to 2–1. Still, by forcing the ball up in the zone, it changed Buhner's line of vision. In other words, it made him vulnerable on the very next pitch to something lower in the strike zone, which is why, when I threw a fastball on the outside corner, barely above his knees, all Jay could do was take it for strike two.

So the last pitch of the at-bat came down to power versus power, a game I knew I shouldn't play too often, especially this late in the game. But I also knew that if I was going to lose this no-hitter, I preferred to know I'd gone down in flames on my best pitch, which at that moment was still my fastball.

All during the at-bat, I noticed an increase in my velocity, which I can only attribute to a surge in adrenaline. My heart was beating so fast, I doubt I would've been aware of a locomotive about to hit me. My mind was focused on one last pitch to Buhner, and I swear the ball that left my hand on the 2–2 count was as small and mean and unhittable as any I've thrown since, well, since 1985.

For one millisecond, I remembered what it felt like to throw a fastball that I just knew a hitter wouldn't touch. It has a special aura to it, one that practically says to a hitter. Go ahead, try to hit me. It's a wonderful feeling, being that bulletproof. I wish I could've gone on forever in my career like that, but for now, I'm thankful I was able to relive it for that one special moment.

That's because I threw that fastball right by Buhner: it was right down the middle, but too powerful for him to handle. I watched as he swung right through, a strikeout that left me just one out shy of that no-hitter. By now, the Stadium was more than electric. It was like some huge, outdoor asylum. With Paul Sorrento standing at the plate, I took one last deep breath, and said a little prayer for my dad, and then for myself. I asked the higher powers to give me the strength to do my very best, at this moment when I needed to remain as focused as possible.

I made my petition in all of a half second, more of a concept prayer than an actual word-for-word utterance. I didn't want to spend too much time doing anything other than concentrating on my last batter, Sorrento, a talented and dangerous left-handed bat.

First pitch: a slider, late-breaking, and too tough for Sorrento to pick up. He saw it at the last second, tried to check his swing, and failed. Strike one.

Second pitch: another slider, since I figured Sorrento would likely be expecting a fastball. It was the right idea, but poor execution. The ball was just off the plate, evening the count to 1–1. Third pitch: here was the same fastball that I'd just thrown past Buhner, but this one was low, and Sorrento, a more disciplined hitter than Jay, didn't go for it. Two balls, one strike.

Fourth pitch: a slider. Why a slider? Because, when thrown to the right spot to a left-handed hitter, usually down and in, the best he'll do is beat it into the ground, usually resulting in a one- or two-hopper at the first baseman.

But there's a great risk factor involved, because as effective as the slider can be to a lefty, it's also that easy to hang it. And that's exactly what I did. In fact, I was horrified at the arc of the pitch, because I knew I'd overthrown it. Instead of having it cut down and in, the ball was floating near the heart of the strike zone, and all Sorrento had to do was time it, meet it, and my no-hitter—and maybe the 2–0 lead—would vanish.

Paul knew it, too. I could see how his eyes widened, ever so slightly, the way every hitter's do when he sees a pitch he can hit. Sorrento was so anxious to crush it, though, he lunged for it—meaning his bat was just a fraction of a second ahead of the pitch's break. And that meant he was under it, hitting the bottom half instead of meeting it squarely.

And *that* meant the gods had just rescued me. Instead of seeing a line drive go screaming into the gap, the ball took off on a huge, lazy pop-up. I looked up and I saw that Jeter was drifting toward the ball, which made me feel good. He was only a rookie, but composed and mature, the kind of player you can trust in a tight spot.

Later on, I heard Jeter telling reporters that he had wanted the ball hit to him. That's the sign of a money player, someone who isn't afraid to meet a challenge. Believe me, there are plenty of talented guys in the big leagues who'd just as soon not be at the plate in the ninth inning with the game on the line, or on the mound with the bases loaded, or standing beneath a towering pop-up that meant the final out in a no-hitter.

The ball stayed up there forever. I swear it felt like slow motion, watching Jeter, his eyes skyward, gloved poised. He took two baby steps to his right, and then I could tell he was ready: the ball fell softly into his glove, and all of a sudden I was totally mobbed by my teammates.

I know Girardi hugged me, so did Wade Boggs, and the rest was a blur of high fives, fists pumping toward the sky, teammates cheering for me, the crowd creating this wild, almost delirious roar. Somewhere in the background, as I was being carried off the field on my teammates' shoulders, I could hear Tina Turner's "Simply the Best" coming from the huge PA system in center field.

I was screaming, tears running off my face, both my hands raised. Every single emotion I could've experienced was running through me at the same time, almost too many for my brain to register. All at once I thought of my dad, of the turmoil in my career, the pain I'd caused my family in the last three years, of the addictions I'd fought, and the places they took me.

I thought about my first time in New York, how I was once part of a team that owned the city. I remember the magic my arm once generated, and how I threw it away. I thought about how lucky I was to have gotten a second chance in baseball, in my career, and how I had made this promise to myself: that I would never, ever take my gifts for granted, ever again.

But mostly, I thought about my father, hoping and praying that he was able to listen to the game on the radio in the hospital. This no-hitter was for him—for all the years of love and guidance he provided, for staying loyal to me even though I'd hurt him so badly by almost getting thrown out of baseball for good.

The postgame press conferences were scores of questions, thousands of answers, all meant to deliver the same message: this game was no coincidence. Not after I'd dedicated it to Dan Gooden, the best friend I ever had, who was just trying to hang on for one more day.

PART III

# BETTER DAYS

# NINE

"SO TELL ME about your family."

That was the first question George Steinbrenner asked me on October 5, 1995. There I was returning to the world of baseball after acting commissioner Bud Selig had ruled against an early reinstatement in the summer of '95. Instead he declared that I was a free agent, able to negotiate with any Major League club, as of October 1.

I'd been flirting with several teams, but it wasn't until two days after the Yankees lost to the Mariners in the division series that I finally collided with the Boss.

Edgar Martinez's game-winning double off Jack McDowell, which scored Ken Griffey all the way from first base, was still rattling around the corner of Seattle's Kingdome, and Steinbrenner had already begun remaking his team.

I have to admit, watching those play-off games, I was rooting against the Yankees. I wanted some of my friends to do well—like David Cone and Darryl, who'd signed with them in mudsummer—but I also knew that a Yankee loss in the play-offs would help me get a job.

I was right, if only because Steinbrenner hated losing to the Mariners and Piniella so much. It must've killed him to be up 2–0 in that best-of-five series, only to drop three straight in the Kingdome.

Although the Yankees lost Game Five, 6–5, in eleven innings, I thought the series turned the Mariners' way when they came back from a 5–0 deficit against Scott Kamieniecki in Game Four. Once Seattle won that game, the Yankees lost whatever advantage they'd had in the first two games.

That meltdown, I believe, is what pushed George to look for new pitchers, which is why he was courting me. All summer, as I worked out at Eckerd, scouts kept showing up with their radar guns and notepads and cell phones; the White Sox were there, as were the Marlins and the Red Sox. But the Yankees obviously intrigued me. Suddenly it didn't matter how much I hated the Pinstripes when I was a Met. Going back to New York was what mattered most, and if the Mets were no longer interested in me, what better way to prove them wrong than by playing for Steinbrenner?

When Ray told me that George had agreed to sit down with me, I was as nervous as the first day I'd ever pitched in the big leagues. I'd known Steinbrenner in a peripheral way through the years; we both were based in Tampa and every so often we'd end up on the same flight home. But like most outsiders, I saw George through the prism of his constant threats against his players, the way he kept firing managers, his lack of understanding that slumps are part of baseball; in a way, they make the sport real.

God, how we used to laugh at the Yankees at Shea a decade earlier. Our attitude was, Fuck the Yankees. Even in spring training we wanted to beat them, and we rooted for them to lose one hundred games a year. This was true even though the guys respected Don Mattingly and Dave Winfield—especially when the two of them were chasing the American League batting title in 1985. Straw had a particular liking for Mattingly. He'd tell me, "That guy just goes about his business, like a real pro. You never see him making any trouble for anyone." But there wasn't much else about the Yankees we could relate to. Certainly not Billy Martin—he could've never handled the Mets.

Still, I'd heard that Steinbrenner had been mellowing in recent years, which made it easier for me to get comfortable with the idea of someday pitching for him. Instead of blasting the Yankees after their loss to the Mariners, George merely told reporters, "There are going to be some changes here."

He wasn't kidding: Buck Showalter, the manager, and Gene Michael, the general manager, were out within a month, replaced by Joe Torre and Bob Watson. Steinbrenner would trade for two of the Mariners who helped sink the Yankees in the play-offs, first baseman Tino Martinez and reliever Jeff Nelson. And Steinbrenner also signed free agent Kenny Rogers that winter, a seventeen-game winner from Texas who had one of the meanest left-handed curveballs in the American League.

No doubt, Steinbrenner was building another golden era in the Bronx, and that was his agenda in meeting me. We agreed to have lunch at Iavarone's, a restaurant near the Yankees' spring-training complex in Tampa. Steinbrenner showed up with Billy Connors, his pitching adviser, who I assumed was part of the Yankees' brain trust. I also assumed this was going to be a contract negotiation, or at least a preliminary one, which is why I was ready to talk pitching, money, or the Mets. Whatever questions Steinbrenner had, I was ready with answers.

Incredibly, though, George never asked me about any of those topics. Instead, he asked me about recovery, the Little League team

I played for in 1975—George swore he remembered seeing me at third base—and about shipbuilding and life in New York. He asked me how I liked coaching my son's team, if I'd seen any good movies, if I'd discovered any new restaurants in Tampa, if I was enjoying my lunch.

Everything except baseball. And I respected that. It made me feel Steinbrenner was interested in me, my life. At the end of lunch, he asked pointedly, "What happens when you have the urge to do drugs? How often do you get them? And what do you do about it?"

I told him I had a support system in place; I'd either call Ray or Ron Dock, and they'd talk me through it. I told Steinbrenner I regularly attended NA meetings now, and that I was finally in my element, surrounded by real-life addicts who were struggling just like me.

Steinbrenner looked at me a moment, then said, "I have a relative who had a problem with alcohol, so I understand what addiction is all about. I know how it can ruin a life, but what I respect about you is that you haven't given up. You've worked very hard to regain control of your life."

And with that, Steinbrenner pushed his plate back, as both he and Connors prepared to leave the restaurant. Not once did we mention a possible contract, or how the Yankees had lost to the Mariners, or what his plans were for me. In retrospect, I think Steinbrenner was testing my mettle, to see if I would finally blurt out, "Are you going to sign me or what?"

That's when I learned what a skilled businessman he was. I was the one who should've been in the driver's seat—after all, the Yankees were desperate for pitching; I had other teams interested in me—yet it was George who dictated the tempo and the subject matter of this meeting. As we shook hands in the parking lot, I thought I'd failed this unacknowledged audition.

"We'll be in touch," Steinbrenner said pleasantly. And then he drove away.

For the next three days neither Ray nor I heard a word from the Yankees. I was starting to think Steinbrenner had agreed to the meeting only as a courtesy to Ray.

I was also moving closer to the conclusion that it'd be wiser to take the Marlins up on their offer, stay close to home, and finally be teammates with my nephew Gary. At least I knew they wanted me; not only did Florida send scouts to see me at Eckerd, but they brought me, Ray, and my father to Miami.

I worked out for them in the bullpen prior to a game, and then I sat in owner Wayne Huizenga's private box while the Marlins got crushed. Their pitchers combined to surrender ten runs. All the pieces fit together perfectly.

And unlike Steinbrenner, Huizenga made no secret of his interest in signing me. Instead of a distant "nice meeting you" at the end of the night, he enthusiastically said, "Can't wait to have you here next year, Doc."

I was so impressed with Huizenga's energy, and a subsequent offer of $1.5 million, I told Gary Carter, who was then working as a color commentator for the Marlins, "This is where I want to be." In fact, had Steinbrenner not called for a second meeting within a day or two, I doubt I would've waited any longer.

But just as Ray kept telling me, Steinbrenner indeed broke his silence and said he wanted to offer me a contract at a meeting at the Bay Harbor Inn, the hotel he owned on Tampa Bay. This time Steinbrenner brought his attorney, David Sussman. I brought my father and Ray. Steinbrenner's tone was entirely different this time. He was all business and had obviously prepared his sales pitch.

"Dwight, there's no team in baseball that can match the Yankees for history and tradition," George said. "I want you to be part of that; I think you can be a Yankees pitcher for a long time. I know you've talked to other clubs, the Marlins for instance. Go out and compare the offer they've given you with what I'm about to suggest. Let's see if we can work this thing out."

As it turned out, the Yankees offered me base salaries of $1 million in 1996, $2 million in 1997, and $3 million in 1998, with the club holding the option for both '97 and '98. There were incentives, tied mostly to the number of innings I pitched—which I thought was fair enough, considering I hadn't thrown a full season since 1992.

After telling George I found the base salaries to be acceptable, I asked for—and got—a $300,000 payout if Steinbrenner decided not to exercise the option in either of the two subsequent years. We were just about to shake hands on the contract when Steinbrenner stared me in the eye and offered some steely advice.

"I've decided to take a chance on you, but don't you ever fuck me," he said. I was shocked at his profanity, but it sure hit home. "Don't embarrass me, don't make me or the Yankees look bad, or I promise you'll be sorry you ever met me."

Then Steinbrenner paused and asked, "Are we clear on that, Dwight?"

I nodded. He offered his hand, which I accepted. I had become a Yankee.

I REMEMBER THE very first time I put on the pinstripes; it was on the first day of pitchers and catchers in spring training in 1996. The moment I'd finished dressing, something strange happened to me: I felt stronger, more confident, like I could throw the ball harder than at any time in my career. Is this what everyone meant about the Yankee uniform—that it was such a psychological booster shot, it could actually make you play better?

All these years I thought it was just hype. But it was true. I felt more professional than I ever did in a Mets uniform. Everything about the Yankees was rich and crisp and properly executed. They had a bigger clubhouse, more clubhouse attendants, more coaches to run more drills, more equipment, even more security guards. On my very first day I was seduced.

Looking around the clubhouse, I realized also it'd been years since I'd been surrounded by so much talent. The '96 Yankees were clearly play-off contenders, one could see that even before we'd played an inning.

The pitching staff was loaded; there was Cone, Jimmy Key, Andy Pettitte, Kenny Rogers, and me. In fact, the press was already drawing comparisons between the '96 Yankees' rotation and that of the 1986 Mets. It was a tough pick, because there were so many similarities.

I mean, Cone was older and wiser as a Yankee, but no less effective. Kenny Rogers reminded me of Sid Fernandez, with that funky delivery, Jimmy Key was like Bobby Ojeda, smart and able to think along with a hitter, pitch by pitch. And Pettitte was a left-handed Ron Darling, somehow always able to win.

It was a close call. As for me . . . well, no one expected me to be the Doctor K of the eighties. In fact, no one around the Yankees really knew what they were getting. Even though I'd pitched effectively in a brief stint in the Puerto Rican winter league just after signing with the Yankees, the truth was, I was coming off an 18-month layoff and hadn't had a winning season since 1991.

The other unknown factor was that I had to learn an entire league, most of them hitters with whom I was unfamiliar. That meant new umpires, new strike zones, and, of course, the designated hitter. It wasn't going to be easy, but I was determined to prove to the world that George Steinbrenner had made the right decision signing me.

I mean, it would've been so easy to turn his back, say there wasn't any room. Steinbrenner had taken a chance on Straw in the second half of the 1995 season, but for some reason hadn't asked him to return in 1996. So, obviously, there was a limit to how many risks the Boss was going to take. But now it was my turn, and I felt like I had good stuff going into the spring training season.

My fastball felt live enough, that was sure. The very first day we were throwing off the mound, Cone said, "Christ, you're making me feel like I'm around eighty miles an hour." I had a head start on the other pitchers; that much was true.

But I'd forgotten how wide the gulf was between good stuff off a sideline mound and being able to actually throw the ball past a major league hitter.

I got my reeducation, cold and merciless, when the exhibition season began. To say I got hit hard was an understatement. I had only one solid outing, against the Indians, in Winter Haven. Otherwise I felt I was naked against these hitters—not enough life on the fastball and not enough control of my curveball. Still, Joe Torre showed remarkable patience, never once revealing if he was worried about me. I couldn't have blamed him if he was.

In fact, in my last start before the regular season, I allowed the Pirates eight runs and 14 hits, including three home runs, in just five innings. That raised my spring training ERA to 8.88, which was sure putting pressure on both Torre and Steinbrenner.

To any outsider, I must've looked like I was done. Pirates manager Jimmy Leyland was gracious enough to point out to reporters that the wind at McKechnie Field was blowing straight out, and any fly ball was a potential home run. But I knew better: I still didn't have enough arm strength to compete against the hitters.

In six spring training starts, I allowed forty hits in twenty-five and a third innings, and opponents batted .323 against me. Obviously, I needed more time, but Opening Day was only a week away. And what could I say to reporters, other than that I was still working on things?

To Torre's credit, he called me into his office to say, "You'll be fine. Just trust your stuff, it'll come back." I learned in my first weeks as a Yankee that Torre had a quiet, mature presence. He wasn't like Dallas Green, trying to show up the players, and unlike Buddy Harrelson, Torre had a personality that was big enough for the job. In a sense, Joe was like Davey Johnson, in that he gave his trust freely, as long as you didn't cheat him.

At least Torre was that way with me. But I found it odd the Yankees didn't show Kenny Rogers the same patience that they had with me. I didn't pitch significantly better than Kenny—in fact, my ERA was higher than his, 8.40—but he'd been struck on the back by a Tony Fernandez line drive during batting practice, and never really found his equilibrium after that.

By the end of camp, Torre had decided to leave Kenny in Florida. Kenny was pissed and I didn't blame him. After all, he had just signed a four-year deal worth $20 million, and nowhere in the contract did it say he had to pass a spring-training audition. Rogers had terrific stuff; everyone in baseball knew that, and he once threw a perfect game for the Rangers.

But as much as I admired Kenny for his talent, I also had the sense that we were never going to see his true skills as long as he was a Yankee. Whether it'd be from an elbow injury, or the pressure of coming to New York as a big-money free agent, Rogers just never looked comfortable.

Then again, neither did I. In my first five starts, I was 0–3 with an 11.48 ERA, and all the doubts and whispers that'd been hounding me in spring training were now roaring in my ear. In my very first start since 1994, I lost to the Rangers, 7–2, in Arlington. Thanks to Will Clark's RBI double, I was down 1–0 in the span of just three batters, and I ended up surrendering five runs and five hits, including a solo HR to my old Met teammate, Kevin Elster.

I lost to the Rangers again a week later, then the Twins. I went into May winless, and if there's one thing I learned about the

Yankee universe, it's that patience is a rare commodity. I remember leaving the ballpark one day after a game, crossing the street with Monica to the players' parking lot.

We ran into Steinbrenner, who first made sure he was respectful to my wife.

"Monica, great to see you. How are the kids?" he said pleasantly.

Before she even finished answering him, Steinbrenner had already trained his laserlike gaze on me.

"Hey, you gotta pitch better than that," George said coldly. "I'm giving you ten starts to find out where you are. You understand? Ten."

Since I was 0–3, I thought that meant I still had a cushion. But the mercurial Steinbrenner probably never remembered quoting me that figure, because the very next week I was out of the rotation. For the first time since signing with the Yankees, I was beginning to have doubts about my career. At first, I thought the problem was arm strength. Then I shifted my focus to better location. Nothing was helping. And then I realized I was simply trying too hard.

I wanted the world to know that Dwight Gooden—Doctor K—was back. But that wasn't all. I wanted to make Steinbrenner look good; I could only imagine how many people were laughing at him now, because of me. Conversely, I also wanted to make the Mets look bad and prove to all those judgmental people out there that *everyone* deserves a second or third chance, or as many as he or she needs, as long as they're still giving an honest effort at their vocation.

With such a long to-do list, no wonder I was getting my butt kicked. I was on the mound overthinking, and choking off my natural ability. I can still hear the instructions I was barking in my own head: Keep the arm up, weight back, push off the right leg, follow through.

I tried to follow everyone's advice, which meant I was adhering to none of it. Truth was, I was miserable, and when Mel Stottlemyre told me Joe wanted me to miss a turn and go into the bullpen, I was grateful. I was in long relief, which essentially meant I'd become invisible to the Yankees.

One day in late April, we were in Milwaukee and Ray approached me after having had a discussion with our general manager, Bob Watson. Ray was assigned to be my liaison, counselor, buddy, you name it and Ray helped me out, especially on the road. He was getting paid by the Yankees to help me keep my head straight, which is undoubtedly why Watson raised this sensitive topic through my friend.

Would I accept a demotion to Class AAA Columbus?

I immediately said no. If my standing with the Yankees had fallen so precipitously, then I preferred to be released outright. There were plenty of major league teams that were looking for pitching, and would've been willing to experiment on a former Cy Young Award winner who was only thirty-two.

But to go to the minor leagues—even for, "just a start or two," as Watson had promised Ray—would've been giving the Yankees the license to bury me.

Think of it: if I pitched well in the International League, it would've been only because I was supposed to. But if I let those Class AAA kids light me up, the Yankees would have every reason to keep me there for a month or two or three, and when they finally released me, there's not a team in either league that would've signed me.

So I instructed Ray to tell Watson and Torre that I wasn't going anywhere, that if the Yankees wanted me out of their faces, they'd have to do it the hard way. So they backed down, and I remained in the bullpen for nine days, completely off the radar screen, feeling less and less like a Yankee every single game.

It's easy to see how a player can drift away from his teammates if he isn't playing much. He still jokes and laughs with the guys, but without the sense that he's contributing, he becomes an outsider. Yet, as removed as I felt from the Yankees, I also came upon a revelation: if I wasn't going to win the Cy Young in 1996, the least I could do was enjoy myself.

Isn't that why I fell in love with baseball in the first place, because it was fun? Because I was good at it, and people enjoyed watching me? All I wanted was to recapture that fun again. I decided it wouldn't matter if it lasted a week or a day, or even just an inning. But I wanted that rush one more time. Once I decided that, I felt a weight had been lifted off my shoulders. That was one key element of my rebirth in 1996. The other was a slight alteration in my delivery, thanks to a suggestion from Mel.

Until now, my windup had always been long and complicated—an unusually high kick, with a coiling and uncoiling of the left leg and sometimes exaggerated follow-through. That worked fine when I was young and my limbs were a little thinner; over the years I became more thickly muscled and found it harder, and not as necessary, to kick my leg that high.

But I never thought to completely economize my motion until one day in the bullpen. Mel asked me if I remembered the last five warmups I used to take after the national anthem in the bullpen at Shea. In a rush to get to the mound, I barely wound up; instead I kept my delivery to a minimum, and Mel—one of the few pitching coaches who actually catches his pitchers—said, "Those were always your best fastballs, because you weren't overthrowing them."

So Mel turned back the clock: he suggested I officially adopt the hurry-up windup, which eliminated me raising my hands over my head. Instead, I took the ball out of my glove almost immediately and reduced the overall movement I needed to deliver the ball.

Mel said, "Why don't you think about using that delivery next time you're out there?" He was nodding toward the mound on the field, but, of course, he couldn't tell me when that'd be. Only

Torre knew, and it appeared that I'd permanently lost my rotation spot.

That is, until the day when Cone started feeling an odd tingling in his right hand, almost as if the fingers were going numb. Cone told me he was a little freaked out by it, because it was unlike any pitching-related injury he'd ever suffered.

Doctors admitted him to Columbia Presbyterian Hospital, which was bad news for him and the Yankees, but it gave me a chance for a second audition. I took Cone's start against the Twins on April 27, and even though I got a no-decision in an 8–6, ten-inning loss, I felt like a different pitcher. I allowed Minnesota only five hits and one run in six innings, and afterward, Paul Molitor told reporters, "That was a much better fastball that Doc had."

He was right. The ball felt smaller in my hand, and suddenly I had arm speed again. Could the elixir have been the windup? Just that? Stottlemyre always said that the difference between pitching on the side and throwing in a game is adrenaline. I had it again. I was back, after all . . . after I finally stopped trying to announce it.

On May 8, I won my first game in almost two years, beating the Tigers, 4–2, and now all my weapons were at my disposal.

Six days later I was standing on the mound against the Mariners in Yankee Stadium.

DID I KNOW the 1996 Yankees were on their way to the World Series? I could tell early on how good we were, but it was just as obvious to me that the Orioles were going to stay close to us that summer. The rotation suffered a serious setback when it was discovered that Coney had an aneurysm in his right shoulder and would be out for most of the season. That put added pressure on Jimmy Key—who was returning from shoulder surgery of his own in 1995—Rogers, Pettitte, and, of course, me.

By May, I was a completely different pitcher than the one who was getting his butt kicked in spring training. I had better arm strength, better location, but mostly I was finally starting to relax and believe that I belonged in the American League. The irony is that it took Cone's injury to provide me with a chance; had he not gone on the disabled list, it's possible I would've been released within the next few weeks.

Instead, I started to resemble the pitcher I once was with the Mets. Over my next twenty-one starts, I was 11–2 with a 3.51 ERA, which proved my critics wrong and, most importantly, paid George Steinbrenner the professional dividend he deserved.

Being a Steinbrenner employee was a unique experience—absolutely, unconditionally, the opposite of what it meant to be a Met in the eighties. You could always tell the difference at the Stadium when George was in the ballpark and when he was in Tampa.

When Steinbrenner was around, the employees were incredibly uptight; even the security guards at the front door of the clubhouse had this worried expression. Everyone was paranoid about getting fired.

In late summer, we signed Wally Whitehurst, a right-hander who spent a few good years with the Mets and was now bouncing around from team to team. Wally came straight from the old days of anarchy at Shea and had no idea how different life was in the Bronx.

In fact, one day during batting practice, he asked me, "What time does the pizza get here?" It was a common practice among the Mets to order a pizza right before game time. I looked at him and said, "Wally, we don't do that shit here." He looked at me like I was speaking Greek.

All the fear flowed from the top, and I can't say that fear was unfounded. In fact, when I was finalizing my deal with Steinbrenner in October in Tampa, I had my first exposure to his legendary rage. Our talks at the Bay Harbor Inn were running long, and it appeared I was going to miss a flight back to New York. I told Steinbrenner I was worried about that, and he picked up the phone to call his secretary.

"Tell the driver I've arranged for Gooden to go over to the airport and see if there's a later flight," he said.

A few minutes later the secretary called back to say, "The driver said he can't find any flight information over there. He doesn't see anything on the monitor."

George's eyes widened immediately. I could see he was squeezing the phone in anger.

"Well, tell him he's fired!" he shouted. "Go get me someone who can read!"

And just like that, Steinbrenner hung up, looked at me, and pleasantly said, "Now, Doc, where were we?"

I was shocked that George could separate a man from his livelihood so easily, but as I was to learn, those moments of rage came and went quickly. After they evaporated, the fired employee would almost always get his job back.

But that didn't seem to ease anyone's day-to-day tension. Steinbrenner had a hand in every aspect of the Yankees' operation. Example: Andy Pettitte had been experiencing some lower-back pain that summer, which prompted Steinbrenner to order a massage. In his next start, Andy threw a shutout—which was great for his confidence, but it created a personal hell for the trainers.

That's because George now required *every* pitcher have a massage before he took the mound. The scene was pathetic: the trainers, Gene Monahan and Steve Donahue, were reduced to begging pitchers to come lie on the massage table, because they knew failure to comply would evoke George's wrath against *them,* not the players.

"Doc, please, just two minutes," Donahue said to me one day before I was scheduled to start.

"Steve, sorry, can't do it," I said, trying to keep a straight face.

"We'll just pretend you're getting massaged," he said, his panic quotient now rising. "We don't even have to go through with it."

"Nope."

"Doc . . . please," Donahue pleaded.

It went on like this all summer. Steinbrenner also required that everyone be weighed constantly; he was obsessed with how we looked in our uniforms. That meant the trainers were doubly worried about their jobs. In fact, I'd say Monahan and Donahue had the most unforgiving day-to-day existence in the organization, because one of them always had to be on standby to take a Steinbrenner phone call.

If you ever look carefully into the Yankee dugout during a game, you'll never see both trainers present. That's because one of them is always in the trainers' room, ready to answer questions in case George—who's watching the game from somewhere, either in the ballpark, or on TV in Tampa—wants to know why this guy looks tired or slow.

But I will say this about Steinbrenner: he gives the Yankees every opportunity to win, and doesn't care how much it costs. Unlike some owners, who invest in their teams only to make a profit, George's primary concern is winning, and there isn't a player in the big leagues who doesn't respect that. Not only will Steinbrenner spend money on free agents, but he'll spend to make sure every baseball we use for practice is brand-new. Big things and little things, too. That's what commitment means.

Of course, being among the elite tends to foster resentment, and I found that while National League teams hated the Mets personally in the eighties, beating the Yankees was even more satisfying to American Leaguers. Every team treated a series with us like the World Series; I'd never seen so much adrenaline expended in the middle of a regular season.

I saw that in particular in games against the Mariners, Red Sox, and Orioles, and to a slightly lesser degree, the Rangers, too. The American League was a haven for big offense, unlike anything I'd ever seen in the National League. Unlike the NL, whose teams usually had one or two long-ball threats—three, tops—the American League lineups were loaded with power.

Part of the difference was the designated hitter, of course. And the ballparks in the American League tended to be smaller. But the hitters were also helped by a tighter strike zone and the umpires' unwillingness to call a third strike, particularly on the league's best hitters.

I had trouble understanding that, especially since in the NL, pitchers routinely get hitters looking at a third strike. Watch Greg Maddux one day, and see how much he'll expand the strike zone during the course of an at-bat. So much so that his strikeout pitch is sometimes three to four inches off the plate. I received no such courtesy in the AL. It wasn't hard to get to two strikes, but guys like Ken Griffey Jr. and Mo Vaughn had to swing through strike three for me to punch them out. No way would most umpires ring them up.

The result is that AL hitters usually had the luxury of zoning the pitches to their liking, not mine. That only made them more aggressive, and that's led to them crowding the inside corner. The only defense for a pitcher is to brush a hitter back or even knock him down occasionally. That's just part of baseball's way, part of the way a pitcher works a hitter. I don't believe a pitcher should ever deliberately throw at a batter, that's wrong. But if you give away the inside corner, you're done.

I mean, a pitcher *has* to have an intimidation factor working in his favor. It's the first lesson I learned from my father when we used to watch Bob Gibson on TV. But pitchers seem to have lost their courage. Now hitters step out on them, they make you wait, they put on a show for the crowd at your expense. Any batter who steps out when a pitcher has already begun his windup *should* get knocked by the very next fastball.

A mature professional hitter will realize that it's nothing personal—the same way no one thinks twice when a line drive comes back at a pitcher's head. In fact, when I first came up, a hitter who was knocked down or brushed back would get his revenge by hitting one back up the middle. Today, hitters have an attitude that's changed the way baseball is played. People ask me all the time: is the pitching worse than it used to be? My answer is no, it's just that the baseball establishment is catering to the guy with the bat in his hands.

If I was eighteeen now, I probably would make more of an effort to develop as a position player, only because the climate is so favorable to hitters. Let's face it, home runs sell. Home runs look great on TV. Home runs bring fans to the ballpark, and especially now that Mark McGwire and Sammy Sosa captured an entire nation in 1998, it's obvious Major League Baseball will do everything possible to keep the HRs coming. If it means diminishing the science of pitching, too bad.

AS MUCH AS the American League was in love with power and big-inning offense, the Yankees were lacking in that department. In fact, baseball people were saying that Joe Torre and his bench coach Don Zimmer had brought National League baseball to the Bronx, because we didn't score a lot of runs.

Paul O'Neill and Tino Martinez and Bernie Williams were all enormously talented, but not classic HR guys. We did have Ruben Sierra, who hit eighty-two home runs between 1987 and 1989 in Texas, but he wasn't the hitter he used to be. It was kind of sad, really, the way Ruben kept trying to pull the ball even though pitchers kept working him outside.

He stood too far off the plate, and never really embraced the idea of hitting to the opposite field. I guess he thought it wasn't manly enough. In fact, Ruben's ego is what eventually ended his career with the Yankees when he called Torre a liar. He claimed that Joe had promised that he'd get playing time in left field, only to discover that he was the DH and that Tim Raines and Gerald Williams were getting most of the playing time in left field.

Joe handled the potential crisis quietly. Unlike Tony La Russa, who had similar problems with Sierra in Oakland and ended up calling him "the village idiot," Torre never resorted to name-calling. He just said he was sorry Ruben felt that way, but reminded everyone that, as a manager, he never made playing-time promises to players.

After that incident, it was only a matter of time before Sierra was gone. In fact, Bob Watson's ability to trade Ruben to the Tigers for Cecil Fielder two months later made him, in my mind, the executive of the year. In one swap, we were getting rid of an unhappy, unproductive player in exchange for a real stud. Everyone knew and liked Big Daddy. In fact, when news of the trade circulated around the clubhouse on July 31, I saw guys high-fiving each other. A lot of us believed we won the pennant that very day, just because Big Daddy was now being teamed up with Strawberry, who finally signed with the Yankees on July 4.

It'd been over a year since I saw Darryl, and I couldn't believe how good he looked, how happy he seemed, like all those old demons were finally defeated. He'd come a long way since the previous summer, when I went to visit him at Steinbrenner's Bay Harbor Inn in Tampa. Darryl had just signed with the Yankees for the first time and he was getting himself into shape with the minor leaguers.

It was a nice comeback story, albeit a complicated one. Darryl had been convicted of a tax felony in April 1995, and besides the penalty and fines he had to pay, he was also ordered to spend six months under house arrest. That meant Straw could only go to the stadium, to church, and to his counseling session. Otherwise, he was stuck in the hotel, chaperoned by Arthur Richman, one of Steinbrenner's most trusted lieutenants.

Of course, I was in no position to pass judgment, because I was out of baseball in 1995 on a drug suspension. But when Vincent and I went to visit Darryl, I found him to be distant, preoccupied, almost like he was in a trance.

Maybe he was feeling smothered; there were layers of security around him, and it took half an hour of telephone calls to his probation officer in California just to get into the hotel to see him. Even when we got upstairs, we found a guard at his door.

That might've explained why the fire was gone from Darryl's eyes. Why he was listening to gospel music on the little radio near the bed. Why he just kept repeating, "I'm just thankful to be here." The real Darryl I knew and loved had that charisma, that sense of invincibility that made him such a great hitter—although, sadly, it was part of his decline, too.

Eventually, Strawberry would strike a balance between his ego and his remorse. Certainly, he paid for his mistakes, and I challenge anyone who said he didn't deserve to keep playing baseball. Nowhere in the government's case against him was it stated that Darryl should be unemployed. He pleaded guilty, set up a schedule to repay his fines, remained drug-free from 1995 forward, and conformed to the rules of his house arrest. What else was expected of him?

Darryl could still hit, and the Yankees still needed him. The equation was that simple. Yet so many people were ready to say he didn't belong in the big leagues—that he had forfeited his right to play baseball. The same verdict was handed down on Steve Howe, who I became close friends with in the first half of the '96 season.

Until then, I'd known only that Howe had had seven relapses

in a long, long battle with cocaine addiction, and that most of the public had stopped supporting him. I have to admit, even I wondered how many chances a guy deserved—until I realized that Steve never stopped getting back on his feet and trying.

If I needed two chances, and Darryl needed three, who was really keeping score on Howe, as long as he was still giving the Yankees an honest effort? As Ron Dock taught me, there are different degrees of addiction, and Howe's just happened to be particularly severe. But it didn't make him any less of a human and less deserving to earn a living.

He was actually a very good pitcher; on his good days, Howe could reach 91 mph on the radar gun, which made him a unique setup man for Mariano Rivera and John Wetteland, a lefty with a great fastball. But the fans were merciless; even Yankee loyalists refused to give Howe a break. He told me one day, "These people are eventually going to run me out of town, but don't ever let them do that to you. Stay strong."

Howe was right, of course. Midway through the '96 season, the Yankees released him, and Steve's career pretty much self-destructed soon after, when he was arrested for walking through a metal detector at Kennedy Airport with a pistol. Apparently, the gun belonged to his wife, and she'd forgotten it was packed, but no major league executive was willing to give Howe the benefit of the doubt any longer.

For now, Darryl and I were the spokesmen for second chances. We both knew how closely we were being watched, and since I was there first in 1996, I believe the fact that I remained clean and pitched reasonably well—at least after my 0–3 start—led to Steinbrenner's agreeing to sign Straw.

It would've been a perfect full-circle story for the two of us, except that my arm didn't comply. By late August I was starting to run out of gas, having spent the entire summer of 1995 working out and auditioning for scouts, then playing winter ball in Puerto

Rico, after which I began pitching at the Yankees' Tampa complex in January. I'd been throwing nonstop for almost a year and I was finally paying the price for that workload.

It's the most helpless feeling, knowing your fastball has deserted you, and yet being unable to fix it. I tried working with weights, I tried rest, and none of it seemed to help. For the first time in my career I was lost as to what the next step should be.

I certainly didn't want to hurt the Yankees, because we were in a dogfight with the Orioles. But I couldn't deny that I no longer had my best stuff. There was a three-game stretch in mid-September during which I had a 12.54 ERA, and on September 27, after allowing the Red Sox six runs and eight hits in five innings, the Yankees decided to take me off the postseason roster.

It was a bitter disappointment, because I'd worked so hard to help the Yankees—and to reclaim my own career. I had so much to prove to myself, my family, and my fans. But as a professional athlete, I couldn't let my ego eclipse the reality that, if I kept going to the mound with a diminished fastball, I would continue to get my butt kicked.

That put me in the strange position of being a cheerleader for my own team, and an observer of the Yankee Stadium, postseason experience. I'd always heard from American League players that there was nothing like walking into the Stadium before a big game. There isn't a louder, more energetic, and, often, more hostile crowd anywhere in baseball.

Met fans made plenty of noise in the eighties, there's no mistaking that. But it didn't compare to the intensity of a Yankee gathering. Standing in the outfield during batting practice before Game One of the Division Series against the Rangers, I could've sworn this was a hockey or football game I was attending. David Cone said to me, "There's a real edge to this crowd," and I could see what he meant. It bordered on violence.

Not that we minded, certainly not as the home team. But I

could tell the Rangers were unsettled by it. Jeff Nelson said that in 1995, while warming up the bullpen as a Mariner, a fan poured a full cup of beer over him, without fear of being caught or punished.

"There were no cops out there," Nelson said incredulously. "You try not to let it bother you; you don't want the fans to think you're intimidated. But a lot of teams' relief pitchers don't go out to throw unless they're specifically told to warm up."

As it turned out, we needed all the help we could get from the crowd, because Texas beat Cone in Game One, 6–2, thanks to Juan Gonzalez's three-run HR and Dean Palmer's two-run blast in the fourth inning. Texas had Andy Pettitte down 3–1 in the second inning of Game Two, and since it was just a best-of-five series, I was worried that we'd be cooked early.

We got lucky, though, because Palmer's throwing error on Charlie Hayes's grounder in the twelfth inning gave us a 5–4 win. We swept Texas in the next two games in Arlington and then blew out the Orioles in five games in the League Championship Series.

That's when I started to really believe the '96 Yankees were destined to be champions. We flattened a very talented Baltimore team, scoring six runs in the third inning of the final game. My favorite moment, though, came in Game Four, when, in the course of an 8–4 rout, Strawberry hit two home runs. He crushed three in the entire series, proving once again what a determined man can do, given the chance.

I felt a little bad for Davey Johnson, because the Orioles were his former team, and coming back to manage at Camden Yards meant so much to him. But we had our own managerial subplot going, since Joe Torre's brother, Frank, was in the hospital awaiting a heart transplant, and with each passing day you could see the strain on Joe's face.

We liked Joe, all of us. But more important, we respected him. He never once brought his personal problems into the clubhouse, even though we would've all understood. Hell, there's not a ballplayer alive who hasn't played at least one game with his mind somewhere else—a sick child, an argument with a spouse, or just plain weariness from a 162-game schedule.

But Torre—who'd never been to the World Series in fourteen years of managing the Mets, Braves, and Cardinals—remained an island of calm. In fact, not even Steinbrenner seemed to be able to get under Joe's skin, which might've been a first-ever. One day during the summer Torre stood in the middle of the clubhouse, held up a piece of paper, and said, "Just so you guys know, this is the lineup George wants me to use today."

He read the names. One of them was Ruben Sierra's.

Of course, Ruben had been traded to Detroit a month earlier, which is why we laughed so hard a few of us had tears in our eyes. For the most part, though, we were an incredibly self-contained group, proving an old axiom that says a team reflects the personality of its manager. That couldn't have been truer of the '96 Yankees.

In fact, the only emotional player in the clubhouse was Paul O'Neill, who'd throw his helmet and bat, much the same way as Gregg Jefferies had done. But unlike Jefferies, who many teammates thought was only concerned with his stats, O'Neill is driven by his desire to win. I respect that about him, although I never could understand why a hitter could think he should reach base in every single at-bat, or take issue with every called strike.

Still, O'Neill's fury drove us in the World Series against the Braves, the National League's elite team. They had the legendary pitching staff—who could ever bet against Greg Maddux, John Smoltz, or Tom Glavine?—and after we came apart in Games One and Two, it looked like our ride was over.

In fact, there were rumors that the Braves were really celebrating in the visitors' clubhouse after the second win, telling each other we didn't belong on the same field with them.

They'd outscored us, 16–1, and we were playing the next three games in Atlanta.

After we heard about the Braves whooping it up, it only made us more determined to stick it in their faces. Of course, it was David Cone who shut the Braves down in Game Three, a 5–2 win in which he outpitched Tom Glavine. The turning point, though, was an 8–6, ten-inning win in Game Five, when Jim Leyritz clocked a three-run HR off Mark Wohlers.

Wohlers came into the game needing just six outs to preserve a 6–3 lead. The Braves had ambushed Kenny Rogers for five runs in two innings, but Brian Boehringer, David Weathers, and Jeff Nelson combined to limit Atlanta to just one run over the next five innings. Meanwhile we closed to within 6–3, setting up the most dramatic at-bat since . . . well, I can't remember much better theater.

Understand this about Leyritz: he loves the spotlight, loves attention, and mostly, he loves himself, which isn't altogether a bad thing. You just have to see him in the right light. But guys told me Buck Showalter hated Leyritz and it was pretty obvious that Torre wasn't crazy about him, either.

But none of that seemed to bother Leyritz, who told us in the dugout, "I'm gonna hit one out" against Wohlers. That was no small prediction, considering Jimmy was coming off the bench cold, as a pinch hitter, and Wohlers was throwing close to a hundred miles an hour. The biggest mistake he made was throwing Leyritz a slider with two strikes, which allowed his bat to catch up. A pitcher never wants to lose a game on his second-best pitch, and I'm sure Wohlers hasn't stopped regretting it to this day.

That's because Leyritz hit a monstrous three-run HR, tying the game and setting the stage for Wade Boggs's bases-loaded walk off Steve Avery in the twelfth. That comeback changed the chemistry of the whole series; certainly it stripped the Braves of that confidence they had early on.

In fact, the very next night, Andy Pettitte pitched one of the finest World Series games I'd ever seen, right there with Jack Morris's ten-inning shutout of the 1991 World Series, when the Twins beat the Braves, 1–0. Pettitte outdueled John Smoltz, 1–0, and the mighty Braves were on their way back to New York—swept three straight by the club that didn't even belong on the same field with them.

ANY DIME-STORE PSYCHOLOGIST could see the Braves wanted no part of returning to the Bronx for Game Six. The very fact that manager Bobby Cox delayed the arrival of the team bus as long as possible that day spoke volumes: the Braves were uncomfortable even setting foot in the big Stadium, and felt the longer they were exposed to the hostile crowd the greater the chance they'd wilt.

Still, we knew there wouldn't be much of a window, not with Maddux pitching. If there was any chance of winning Game Six, it would have to be early. But there was a greater karma working in our favor that night, because we learned that Frank Torre had finally received a new heart and underwent a successful transplant only hours before we took the field.

Was there any doubt this was our moment in history? We scored three runs in the third inning, including Joe Girardi's line-drive triple to right center that must've stunned Maddux. O'Neill, who'd led off the inning with a double to right and had moved to third on Mariano Duncan's grounder to the right side, said that when he was crossing the plate, giving us a 1–0 lead, "I swear I could feel the ground shaking."

That's how loud the Stadium was.

Jimmy Key ended up outpitching Maddux, and with help from Rivera and Wetteland at the end, we beat the Braves, 3–2. That last out was so, so sweet: with Marquis Grissom on first, Wetteland got Mark Lemke to pop up to Charlie Hayes behind third base—an almost identical finish to the way the Yankees beat the Red Sox in that one-game playoff in 1978.

That's when Goose Gossage got Carl Yastrzemski to pop out to Graig Nettles for the last out, with everyone in Fenway dying a slow death. This time, though, it was the Braves who were numb with shock, as we mobbed Hayes and Wetteland and O'Neill and just about anyone we could see.

Through the jungle of arms and legs and high fives and slapped backs, I made my way over to Torre and hugged him. I knew how great his burden had been, and how the last twenty-four hours must've been a personal hell, until the doctors told him that Frank would be okay.

The beauty of the '96 Yankees is that we forced people to like us. Even hardened Yankee haters were forced to admit their admiration for Torre, and for the quiet, dignified way we went about our business. I'm sorry I never stepped on the field in October, but I'll always be proud of the contributions I made to that great team.

If nothing else, the '96 Yankees gave me a second chance to make it to a World Series parade. There was *no* way I was going to miss that one, and in a way, it made me even sorrier for the mistake I made in 1986. The parade, which attracted over three million people, was overwhelmingly affectionate and peaceful. It made me realize how strong a hold the Yankees had over the city, and how it must've been in the fifties and sixties, when the Yankees seemed to win every year. In fact, I remember riding on that float down Broadway, feeling the city's love wash over all of us, thinking: I could get used to this.

# TEN

IN A PERFECT world, good teams build dynasties because their players are happy to be part of a winning equation. But the reality is always different. Just two months after the Series, Cecil Fielder demanded a trade, saying he had no desire to share the DH spot with Darryl Strawberry.

I know Cecil was upset that Torre started Darryl against the Rangers' John Burkett in the first game of the Division Series. In fact, Big Daddy said he would "never forgive" Joe for that decision, which I thought was a regrettable thing to say, even though I know it was just Fielder's competitive nature that was speaking.

It was obvious that Torre had faith in Fielder—he did, after all, use him at first base in Game Five of the Series, even though it meant benching Tino Martinez. But that didn't stop Fielder from deciding that he wanted out. He demanded a trade, which was his contractual right, but I don't think Cecil ever stopped to think of the ramifications with the public.

After all, the memory of the World Series was still fresh in fans' minds—one of the most dramatic October comebacks in history—yet here was Big Daddy talking about his own at-bats.

Actually, I understand where he was coming from. Hell, I'd have a problem with a player who'd willingly give up his starting position. The only difference I might've had with Fielder is that I would've made my feelings known privately. I would've gone to Steinbrenner and said, "Maybe it's best for me to move on." That way, it wouldn't look like I was showing the team, or the loyal fans, any disrespect.

But Fielder set the tone for a difficult and contentious season in 1997. The fans never forgave him, and it didn't help matters that he started off slowly in April. Cecil broke his hand sliding into home plate in June, and although he returned in September, Big Daddy never recaptured the magic he created when he first arrived in 1996.

I tried to lighten Big Daddy's mood at one point during spring training. He seemed so sullen and withdrawn, like the contract was the only thing on his mind. So one late morning, as Ray Negron and I were driving to an exhibition game in Bradenton, I had a brainstorm.

"Ray, give me the cell phone. I want to make a call," I said.

Ray handed it to me, then listened while I called the Yankee complex.

"This is George. Give me the locker room," I said, using my near-perfect imitation of Steinbrenner on the unsuspecting switchboard operator. Negron was giggling, sounding like a hyena, because for months he told me I didn't have the balls to ever use the Steinbrenner voice in public. But something in me just clicked, and was ready to accept Negron's dare.

I heard the clubhouse phone ring once, before it was answered by one of the kids working with Nick Priore, the equipment manager. Sounding as impatient and rude as possible, I said, "Yeah, is Fielder still there?"

The kid was a little slow in responding, so I pushed this joke to an even greater absurdity.

"Who the fuck is this?" I shouted.

"Pete," someone said in a small voice.

"Pete, do you still want to have a job tomorrow?"

"Yes."

"Then put Fielder on the fucking phone."

There was a few moments' silence, which told me the kid had fallen for the trick. Both Ray and I were laughing so hard that when Big Daddy finally got to the phone, I could've sworn he heard us.

Instead, all he said was, "Yeah?"

"Cecil? Cecil . . . this is George."

"How're you doing?" he asked cautiously.

"Listen, we've been fighting way too long about this, I think it's time you and I sit down face-to-face," I said. "I want you to be a Yankee for a long time, and I don't see why we can't work this contract thing out."

Now, I fully expected Fielder to break out laughing and tell me I was full of shit. I mean, how could he not know it was me? Did he really believe Steinbrenner was calling him on a car phone, doing an end around on his own agent?

Obviously, Big Daddy did believe me, because he happily said, "George, I'd love to meet with you. Let's do it as soon as possible."

"Fine," I said. "I'll get back to you in a day or two, or maybe I'll just find you in the clubhouse and we'll go up to my office."

"Great. That'd be great."

By this time I was laughing so hard, I was practically convulsing, and nearly drove my Mercedes off the road. I wanted to tell Fielder that I'd just hoaxed him, but he seemed so happy I couldn't break his heart like that. What I hoped for, then, was for the illusion of George's supposed optimism to just fade away; that Big Daddy would just forget about it.

No chance.

What I didn't count on happening was Fielder talking to reporters about his "conversation" with Steinbrenner. It was in all the papers the next day—that he and Steinbrenner were getting ready for this huge summit. That never happened, obviously, and to this day Fielder doesn't realize that "conversation" with the Boss never took place. It was with little ol' me.

Cecil's unhappiness was only one of the reasons the '97 season will be remembered a little less fondly by Yankee fans. The other subplot was the war at third base between Wade Boggs and Charlie Hayes, who were greeted in camp with the news that they'd be fighting for the everyday job.

Neither player appreciated the competition. Hayes was the better fielder, the one who had power in the gaps, but overall I considered Boggs to be the superior offensive threat. There was no way for Torre to please both guys.

Personally, I would've never been able to make a choice between Boggs and Hayes; I would've done exactly what Joe did, which was periodically to change his allegiance based on who was hot at the time. The only thing that bothered me about Boggs was that after he went into a serious slump in May and lost the job to Charlie, he told reporters he was "mentally shot."

To me, that meant Boggs was giving up on the team. If a guy quits on you, I've got a problem with that, especially a veteran. That's when he should be working harder than ever. But to throw your hands up and capitulate . . . I felt Boggs was sending a bad message to the team about himself.

I understood his frustration, but if he indeed quit, which was wrong, then he shouldn't have gotten the job back the rest of the season. It wasn't fair to Charlie.

Other than that, however, I got along with Boggs far better than I anticipated when I joined the Yankees. I'd heard over the years that he was aloof, selfish, eccentric. None of those criticisms were true, except the eccentricities.

One of Wade's "things" was to stand on the top step of the dugout just before the start of the game, waiting for the clock to turn to something with a number 7. I mean, for a 7:35 game, we'd usually run onto the field at 7:37. Or for a 7:05 game, Boggs would have to wait until it was 7:07.

Of course, Kenny Rogers and I had great fun with Boggs's hang-ups. We would deliberately wait until 7:38 or even 7:39 if we were feeling especially cruel on the days we were starting, just to drive Wade crazy. Oh, and he would be insane, too.

"Come on, Doc, you ready? You ready?" Boggs would say at 7:37. He'd be pacing the dugout wildly, and the longer we'd stall, the more upset he'd get.

"Let's go . . . now!" Boggs would say. That's exactly when Boggs *had* to be on the field. Just as Wade *had* to start rocking gently, back and forth, at a certain point during the national anthem. That, and tapping his feet. I don't even think Boggs was aware of that one, but just to be sure, Kenny and I stood on either side of him one night during the anthem, and just when he started rocking, so did we, forming a psycho chorus line.

The other little secret Boggs kept was how strong he was. Everyone thought of him as a high-average contract hitter, which he was. But I'm sure Boggs could've hit thirty HRs a year if he ever put his mind to it. In batting practice, he routinely hit line drives into the upper deck, and I remember one day in 1996, Paul Mastropasqua, one of the team trainers, challenged him

"Wade, this is just BP. You have no power. Nothing. You're weak," said Mastropasqua, who was built like a fire hydrant.

"Weak? Really? Just watch me tonight," Boggs said. In his very first at-bat, he hit a home run, just as he predicted.

But like Fielder, the Boggs-Hayes controversy in spring training was almost eclipsed by yet another breaking story—the Hideki Irabu "Is He or Isn't He Coming to America" drama. That one reached everywhere in the clubhouse, from the veterans who said we didn't need another pitcher, especially a Japanese import who'd never pitched an inning in this country, the younger players, like Andy Pettitte and Mariano Rivera, who had trouble believing that George Steinbrenner was ready to pay a stranger to Major League Baseball several million dollars up front, when they—tried and true Yankees—were still having to fight the Boss for every penny.

I could sympathize with Pettitte and Rivera, but not enough for me to say they deserved raises. I say this even though Irabu received a stunning $12 million contract, $8 million of which was paid up front. Pettitte and Rivera and Jeter didn't have enough service in the big leagues to be eligible either for free agency or arbitration, which meant, in essence, they were at Steinbrenner's mercy.

That was part of the system we all agreed to. For every free-agent millionaire, there are dozens of first-, second-, and third-year players who are underpaid. But we, as players, endorsed this structure, and it was our responsibility to live by it. Personally, I would *never,* and have *never,* asked to renegotiate a contract before its expiration, because that would be going against the deal I originally found acceptable.

I had no hard feelings toward Irabu and his salary. He was a free agent, like anyone else, entitled to make the best possible deal for himself and his family. I was much more interested in learning what kind of pitcher he was than how much money he had in the bank.

After all, we'd heard he was Japan's greatest pitcher ever, capable of throwing a hundred-mile-an-hour fastball and a ninety-mile-an-hour splitter. That was a shocking scouting report, and I told myself: let's just see. I mean, I hoped Irabu was that good. It could only have helped the Yankees to have someone who could throw such an inhuman slider/splitter combination.

But I also came to know that there's no such thing as The Greatest—anything. Irabu was yet another example of that axiom, because (a) he didn't throw anywhere close to a hundred miles an hour, and (b) his splitter, although lively, still bounced in the dirt a lot.

Then again, I was in no position to be critical of Irabu or anyone else. By spring training, I was already in the middle of my own crisis—a hernia that would end up costing me two months of the season. What bothered me so much about this injury was that it was first diagnosed in December, when the trainer at the Tampa complex said it was merely a muscle strain.

The pain never really went away, and I pitched in discomfort throughout spring training and even into the first week of the season. As I was to learn later, the hernia hadn't yet ruptured in the first two months since I felt the pain, but pitching in a live game, against the A's on April 5, I provoked it to blow out completely.

The next morning I woke up in such intense pain, I knew there was something seriously wrong. The Yankees sent me back to New York to be examined by specialists at Columbia Presbyterian Hospital, where it was determined that, yes, I'd had this hernia all along, since December.

Obviously it ticked me off, having been misdiagnosed. If I'd had the injury treated properly back then, I could've been ready to go in spring training, instead of staring at the possibility of missing two months of the regular season, which is what the doctors—including Dr. Stuart Hershon, the Yankees' team physician—were telling me.

In the presence of the other doctors at Columbia Presbyterian, Hershon said it was possible to keep pitching with the hernia, provided I wore a special jock that would keep the muscle wall in my abdomen stable. But that was before a meeting at Yankee Stadium later that same day, this time with George Steinbrenner.

The Boss gathered everyone for a consensus on my injury: GM Bob Watson, trainer Steve Donahue, Dr. Hershon, and me. The meeting got off on a bad note, when Hershon arrived an hour late and said he was delayed by traffic.

Steinbrenner exploded.

"What the fuck do you mean, traffic?" he said. "How many years have you been living in New York, and you still don't leave enough time for traffic? Don't give me your bullshit excuses."

Hershon was clearly intimidated, and I felt that affected the medical advice he subsequently dispensed to Steinbrenner. George went around the room, asking everyone's opinion about whether I should keep pitching and have surgery after the season. Watson preferred surgery now. I obviously wanted to remain active. And Donahue backed me up, saying he thought it was worth the gamble to put off surgery as long as possible.

But when it was Hershon's turn, he panicked, maybe because George was so obviously putting him on the spot.

"What do you say, Hershon?" Steinbrenner said. "You're the doctor, we're going to go on your word. I just don't want this to come back and haunt us. So what do we do?"

Hershon's mouth appeared to go dry, and he swallowed hard. A moment later he blurted, "I think Doc should have the surgery now."

I silently cursed Hershon. But I submitted to surgery a few days later, spent three long weeks recovering at home in St. Pete, then prepared for my return to the Yankees.

Only, it wasn't as simple as that. The front office wanted me to work myself into shape in the minor leagues, which I considered a huge risk. Although I wasn't being sent down for any other reason than for an injury rehab, I still knew what the Yankees would think if I got hit.

Oh, Doc's not ready yet. Let's give it another ten days. And then another. And while you're there, let's get you to work on your curveball a little. I could see it happening, spending most of the summer in Columbus while the Yankees just moved on without me.

And that's exactly what *was* taking place. May turned into June, and I was slowly evolving from a Yankee to a Class AAA pitcher. I wasn't throwing particularly well, either—a decline that was rooted in my depression. I did everything the Yankees asked, showing that I was healthy from the surgery, reaching all my pitch counts, and staying out of trouble, of course.

But that still didn't stir Watson or Torre to summon me—even though, I distinctly remember Watson's last words before I left. He said, "You tell us when you're ready and we'll come get you."

Well, I *was* ready, except now I was tired of waiting for that phone call. So I took matters into my own hands. I approached Ken Schnocke, the Clippers' general manager, and said, "I just got a call from New York. They want me back there. I need you to get me on a flight."

Schnocke was shocked. "I hadn't heard anything like that," he said.

"I'm surprised no one told you, but it looks like I'm gone," I said, furthering this outrageous fib. Schnocke may or may not have believed me, but he wasn't about to call me a liar to my face. So he made the arrangements for me to fly to New York. I arrived at the Stadium in the afternoon, on June 11, before a game against the White Sox. I remember the surprise on Mel Stottlemyre's face when he saw me at my locker.

"Hey, Doc, it's great to see you," he said, puzzled. "I didn't know you were coming back."

With a straight face, I said, "They didn't tell you?"

"No, no one told me anything. Let's see what's what when Joe gets here."

A few minutes later Torre walked in, and we had practically the same conversation.

"Doc, you're here . . . no one told me," he said.

"They told me in Columbus I was being called back to New York," I said innocently. "Do you know when I'm pitching?"

Torre just shrugged. "I haven't heard anything."

I asked him the next day if he had any plans for me to pitch, and he still said no one in the organization knew where to fit me in. So once again I improvised. I saw on the pitching chart that Ramiro Mendoza, who'd taken my spot in the rotation while I was on the DL, was starting Sunday, June 15, in Miami.

So I told Torre the most outrageous lie of all.

"I just spoke to Bob, and he said I'm pitching Sunday."

Torre just shook his head—not in anger toward me, but because in the Yankees' multilayered power structure, no one ever knows what anyone else is doing. Torre was utterly convinced that I'd been returned to him without his prior knowledge, and I took full advantage of that confusion.

Was it was wrong to lie to my bosses? Of course it was. But we were lying to each other. Watson promised I'd be back in the Bronx "when I was ready." But the front office had no intention of doing that, not as long as Mendoza was pitching well, and I had an injury they could keep using as an excuse.

The irony is that my creative thinking paid a dividend. I pitched well enough against the Marlins—five innings, two runs, five hits—to get another start five days later. But that didn't mean everything was fine between me and the Yankees. In fact, the rest of the summer was spent quarreling with Torre about where I fit in the rotation, why I was getting skipped or always pushed back a day or two, and otherwise being treated like a rookie.

I know Torre was still mad at me because of the fistfight I had with a cabdriver in Arlington back in May, when I was still on the disabled list. I knew Joe had stuck his neck out for me, asking that

I be allowed to travel with the team instead of rehabbing in Tampa by myself.

I admit, fighting with a cabbie over a fare was poor judgment on my part, although he did try to cheat me and the incident wasn't entirely my fault. What bothered me more than anything, however, was that Steinbrenner was furious with me. I tried to call him two days before news of the incident became public, but George didn't want to hear my explanation. Instead, he gave me a verbal beating unlike any I've absorbed since I was a kid. And then he hung up on me.

Still, that incident shouldn't have diminished my professional standing with the Yankees. If Steinbrenner and Torre wanted to be disappointed in me personally, they had every right to be. But still . . . why wasn't I pitching?

Why was I the one who was pushed back in the rotation to make room for Irabu's debut after the All-Star break? Why was I the one who was forced to wait six days between starts after beating the Indians on June 20, just so Pettitte—who was roughed up by Cleveland for seven runs in 5.1 innings the next night—could start again on three days' rest?

Torre said it was so Andy could "clear his head." I wonder. Rearranging the rotation like that allowed Pettitte to face the light-hitting Tigers instead of the Indians for a second time in a week. I wonder if the Yankees were trying to protect Pettitte from the Indians. I wonder if he was just ducking them altogether.

All I know is, if that scheduled start had been David Wells's or David Cone's, there's no way either of those two guys would been forced to wait an extra day or two. But I didn't get the same courtesy.

As it turned out, the '97 season ended badly for everyone. After praying and praying not to have to face the Mariners in the playoffs—I couldn't believe how intimidated our hitters were by the prospect of facing Randy Johnson—we ended up losing to the Indians in five games.

Even my final days with the Yankees left a bad taste in my mouth. There'd been some debate as to whether Wells or me should've been the Game Three starter. I actually had no problem with Torre's subsequent decision to use Boomer and put me in the pen; Wells deserved that start, no question. In the postseason you go with the hot hand.

So I was told to be ready for long-relief during the play-offs, which puzzled me because when Cone gave up five runs in the first inning, it was Mendoza who got the call to warm up. I was thinking: I'm supposed to be the fourth starter. I'm the one who has to be used in that situation.

I'm not accustomed to being a reliever, so when Torre brought Mendoza into the game in the second inning, I assumed I wouldn't be pitching in the first round at all. We did win Game One, ironically, on three straight sixth-inning HRs from Tim Raines, Derek Jeter, and Paul O'Neill, but we weren't able to sustain that momentum in Game Two.

That's because the Indians scored five runs off Pettitte in the fourth inning, erasing our early 3–0 lead. Even then, I wasn't asked to warm up. This time it was Brian Boehringer, then Graeme Lloyd and then Jeff Nelson who were used in a 7–5 loss. At this point I was utterly convinced all I was doing was taking up space, which, I guess, was still better than sitting at home watching the games on TV, like so many other players were doing at that moment.

I did see Wells throw a miniature classic in Game Three, a 6–1 win that put us just nine innings away from the League Championship Series. Then, out of nowhere, Torre told me, "You're pitching Game Four."

My reaction was a strange blur of shock, excitement, and anger.

Shock, because I thought Torre had forgotten I was on the roster.

Excitement, because I always pitched well against Cleveland and I was thrilled at the chance to clinch the series for the Yankees.

And anger, because I hadn't pitched in nine days. I hadn't been in my usual, between-starts running-and-stretching programs, thinking every day that I might get into the game as a reliever.

I hadn't done anything that a starter normally does between appearances, because I had to be ready every night for the possibility of a relief appearance.

I felt I was put in a position to fail. In fact, I was pretty sure I was going to get knocked on my ass by the Indians, which would've allowed Torre to say, "Look, this is why we didn't pitch him in the first place."

I'm sure I would've never gotten the ball had Cone not blown out his shoulder. So that night I went back to the Yankees' hotel, worked on my windup in front of the mirror, stretched, tried to focus on individual situations, just to get a feel of what I wanted to do on the mound the next day.

When I finally stood there, in front of a sold-out crowd at Jacobs Field, I took a deep breath and told myself, Whatever happens, happens, so just pitch.

Torre, however, didn't have any such faith in me. In the second inning I gave up a home run to David Justice, and then a double to Matt Williams. I turned around and saw the bullpen was already heating up.

I said, Fuck this; how incredibly disrespectful that was. The thing is, we were leading, 2–1, and I was wondering, Why did Joe even bother to start me? If he was that uncomfortable with me, Mendoza should've taken my spot. Even when I did settle down, Torre couldn't relax.

I remember in the sixth inning, with a runner on first and just after Williams had hit a fly ball to the warning track in center, Joe came to the mound and said, "How are you feeling?"

I told him the truth, that I was fine.

And he said, "Go ahead and finish off the inning. It's yours."

As it turns out, Alomar hit a dribbler down the third-base line, which no one was able to make a play on. And right after that, Torre comes to take me out—after telling me the inning was mine. It's not like Alomar hit a bullet or anything, and we were still ahead, 2–1. I only gave up three hits . . . and yet, Torre no longer had any confidence in me.

It hurt badly to watch us evaporate after that. Mariano Rivera gave up the game-tying HR to Alomar in the eighth, and we ended up losing, 4–3. The next night, the Indians jumped on Pettitte again, and our ninety-six-win season was over. We lost, 4–3, and the pain was so intense, there were guys who openly wept in the clubhouse.

I know Rivera blamed himself for our demise, thinking there must've been some way he could've prevented Alomar's opposite-field HR. I told him, "It's not your fault, man. We would've never gotten close to the play-offs without you."

I knew my words to Rivera were like a good-bye. He might not have understood that, but I did. It was a good and satisfying two-year run with the Yankees, but it was time to move on. The way I was ignored in the second half of the season told me that.

As much as I was going to miss the good guys there—Coney, Straw, Tino, Bernie, Jeter, and of course Steinbrenner, the man who gave me a second chance in baseball—I was already thinking of ways to beat them in 1998.

As an Indian, that is.

## MAY 14, 1996 (continued)

THE FLIGHT FROM La Guardia Airport to Tampa normally doesn't take more than two hours, but on the morning of May 15, 1996, I felt like I was flying to Japan. Part of the reason is that I didn't even sleep an hour the night before. I got home from the ballpark around one A.M., still numb from the postgame celebration. I got a call from George Steinbrenner, and even one from Mayor Giuliani, both of them congratulating me on the best day of my baseball life.

I kept telling them how much I appreciated it, and how much it meant to me, but the truth was, it still hadn't sunk in by the time I got home. I called my mom and then called Monica, talking so fast I didn't even know what I was saying. I was so happy I wanted to explode, but I felt guilty about even smiling, since my dad's condition was still grave.

"How is he?" I asked my mom.

"About the same," she said, which I knew wasn't good news. There wasn't much I could do until I arrived in Tampa, but I still wondered if my dad knew that I'd thrown the no-hitter, and if so, perhaps that gave him enough of a boost to get him through the operation in the morning.

I asked my mom if it was possible he was aware. She said she thought so, but that visiting hours were over before I'd thrown my last pitch. I would definitely have to ask the doctors about that when I arrived.

I wish I could've enjoyed the trip to Florida a little more than I did, because people everywhere were so friendly. At the airport ticket counter, at the gate, and on the plane itself, I got the feeling that everyone was suddenly a Yankee fan.

The amazing thing is that my accomplishments on the baseball field went a long way, I believe, toward helping make up for the mistakes I made in the eighties. It was important that I show New Yorkers that I wasn't through, that I wasn't some washed-up coke fiend, and that I was worthy of their trust and acceptance again.

But those thoughts would be developed on another day, because my universe revolved around St. Joe's Hospital. By the time I walked into the building, it was about eleven A.M., and my father had already undergone the surgery, which began at seven A.M.

I studied the expressions on the faces of my mother, my sisters, and my wife. I had only one question: would Dad be okay? No one knew for sure. The doctors told everyone that he'd survived the operation, but the next few days would be critical. The waiting would be even worse for the family than the days leading up to the surgery itself.

I actually didn't know what to expect when I got to the hospital, but I realized I was as helpless there as I'd been in New York. We spent hours pacing the floor of the waiting room, hoping for some announcement from the doctor. At about two P.M., Steinbrenner arrived at the hospital, a gesture that both surprised and touched me.

It seemed that George had just flown into Tampa for meetings, and having learned that my dad had been operated on in the morning, and that the family was congregated in the waiting room, he dropped everything to pay his respects.

That's the thing about George: he's been tough on a lot of people, and there are reporters who think he's the hardest, meanest SOB in the world. But there's a side to him that reached right into my heart.

"Doc, I want you to know that I'm here to help you any way possible," he said quietly. "I'm not just talking about the Yankees. I'm saying this personally. I'm here as your friend."

George went up to my mother and repeated those exact words. I knew he meant them, too, because if there's one thing I learned about the man, it's that he respects the unity of a family, especially in times of crisis. George didn't spend more than ten minutes with us; he knew we needed to be alone. But his show of support told me I'd made the right choice in signing with the Yankees.

Before he walked out the door, though, George pulled me aside one more time and said, "What you did last night, throwing that no-hitter, I can't tell you how impressed I am."

I started to say something, but George just cut me off.

"I don't mean because we won. You just gave your father the best present he could ever have wished for."

And with that, George walked out the door. If only I knew that he was right. Was it possible that my dad knew that no-hitter—that last, sweet out that fell in Jeter's glove—was his? I needed to know. I brought the no-hit ball with me on the plane, as a gift for Dad. Of course, I didn't dare check it with my bags, and I didn't even store it in the overhead luggage rack on the plane. Instead, I clutched the ball, in my hand, all the way from Roslyn to the waiting room in St. Joe's.

The ball was Dad's. All I wanted was the chance to see him smile one more time. Just once. I wanted him to know what it felt like on that mound, with thousands of people screaming and me thinking of him.

At about five P.M., I finally got my chance to see my dad. The doctors said the anesthesia was finally wearing off and that we'd be able to spend a few minutes in the recovery room with him. I know my mom was very, very anxious to be inside that room, but I asked if I could spend a few minutes with him first. She understood, and squeezed my hand.

I walked into the room, and I was stunned by what I saw. There were so many tubes running out of my dad, there was no way he could speak. He looked small and weak, almost like the operation had shrunk him. I wasn't even sure he was conscious.

I turned to the doctor and asked him if my dad could hear me.

"I think so, Dwight," he said. The doctor smiled and went on, "He could sure hear you throwing that ball last night."

I whirled around, startled.

"He knows about the game?" I asked.

The doctor nodded.

"He knows."

With that, I approached the bed, the ball in my hand.

"Dad," I said.

I looked into his eyes, which were open, but not focused. I could only pray he was listening.

"Dad, I want you to know what I did last night, I did for you. It was for all the years of training, about working hard, for the coaching, for being my buddy, for sticking by me.

"I know I've messed up a lot in my life, I know I've hurt you and Mom. But I want you to know I love you, Dad. I love you both."

I placed the ball in his hand, and whispered in his ear.

"We did it, Dad."

I don't know if he heard me. My father never uttered a word. But as I was about to walk out of the room, I turned around for one last look at him. That's when I noticed a tear running down his cheek.

# EPILOGUE: THE YEAR OF THE TRIBE

AFTER FOURTEEN YEARS of calling New York my baseball home, I finally moved away in 1998. One phone call from the Yankees, and the landscape changed entirely: no more tabloids, or Broadway, the restaurants, and that great, unique energy you only find in the big city.

My contract called for a $3 million salary in 1998, but it also allowed the Yankees the option of not renewing it. In early November, only a few weeks after the World Series, general manager

Bob Watson called to say the Yankees had decided to pass, which turned me into a free agent.

I was disappointed at leaving the Yankees, but not angry and certainly not surprised. Although New York was the only reality I'd ever known in the big leagues, it was pretty obvious I was no longer in the Yankees' future. They needed to make room for Hideki Irabu in the '98 rotation, and with Kenny Rogers still wearing pinstripes, there was simply no room for me.

Still, I left the Bombers with no hard feelings. After all, George Steinbrenner was the one who cleared a path for my return to baseball, and without him, there would've never been that no-hitter or a chance to play on that great '96 team. But I also learned the Yankees weren't the only fit for me.

With the help of my agent, Joseph Ficarotta, and Ray Negron, we shopped around for a new employer, confident that my twenty wins in two seasons in the Bronx would be enough to attract interest. We were right: the Giants, Cubs, Twins, and White Sox all made contact and I'm sure that had we followed up with their preliminary offers and phone calls, I could've been pitching for any of them.

However, there were still two avenues I wanted to explore: the Mets and the Indians. Ever since I signed with the Yankees in the fall of 1995, I'd wondered how my old bosses felt about seeing me in the Bronx. And I also wondered if they were interested in me two years later, after I'd reestablished myself, both as a pitcher and a member of the baseball community.

Free agents don't usually write letters to team owners and general managers; the protocol is that it's the other way around. But I took the time to drop Fred Wilpon, the Mets' owner, a note to tell him I was appreciative of all the good years I'd had at Shea and all the good memories that were still intact, at least for me.

I hoped that would open the door to further dialogue, but Jay Horwitz, the team's publicist and a close personal friend, suggested

I also write to Steve Phillips, the Mets' general manager. Jay said Phillips would be left with the final decision; all Wilpon and co-owner Nelson Doubleday would do is give my return their blessing.

I was a little surprised that Phillips took so long to get back to me: in fact, I had to leave four or five phone messages after my letter, just for him to return my call. And when Phillips and I finally did speak, he said the Mets were looking at other pitchers to fill out their rotation, like Brian Bohanon. Now, Bohanon is a professional pitcher and I mean no disrespect to him, but for Phillips to tell me that was enough to make me shake my head.

Obviously, the Mets must've decided internally not to allow me back to Shea. Maybe it was the dark cloud of the eighties that still hung over the franchise, or the tone of the 1995 *Sports Illustrated* story. If the front office still couldn't digest the history, all Phillips had to do was tell me. I wouldn't presume to think I deserved a spot with the Mets, but I do think I was owed a straight answer.

Instead, I gravitated toward the Indians, against whom I'd pitched so well in 1996 and 1997 as a Yankee. In fact, I never lost at Jacobs Field, which is one reason why Cleveland general manager John Hart pursued me. The Indians fit all the criteria I'd set for myself: they were in a relatively large market with a strong fan base, played in a modern, beautiful stadium, seemed to have good chemistry in their clubhouse, and, as the defending American League champions, they had a legitimate chance to get right back to the World Series.

I could've signed with the expansion Devil Rays—and in some ways, that would've made sense, since they played so close to my home in St. Petersburg. But at this stage in my career, there didn't seem to be any point in going through a rebuilding or a development program. I'd had a taste of winning with the Yankees, and I wasn't about to relinquish that.

So I signed a two-year deal with Cleveland, and I went to spring training with a grand vision of playing an entire season injury-free, showing the Yankees they'd made a mistake letting me go, and pitch in my first World Series since 1986.

This team was absolutely loaded with talent. The starting rotation had Jaret Wright and Bartolo Colon, both of whom were young, hard throwers, along with Charlie Nagy and Chad Ogea. The offense was capable of scoring runs against anyone, since we had Kenny Lofton and Manny Ramirez and Jim Thome and Travis Fryman, and the man who single-handedly ended the Yankees' season in the 1997 American League Championship Series, Sandy Alomar.

What I didn't count on, however, was getting injured in spring training. I wasn't prepared for the different way the Indians asked their pitchers to strengthen their arms, as we threw three days in succession at the opening of camp. After that, we would throw batting practice every other day, receiving only one day's rest in between.

I was accustomed to taking my time in February and March, climbing a much more deliberate arc toward Opening Day. This slower approach was important to me, because, after all, I was in my thirties, and still wary of injuring my shoulder again.

But three weeks into camp, my biceps tendon was again inflamed, just as it was at the end of the 1996 season. The pain was so intense, I had to remove myself from an exhibition game and tell the Indians that I wasn't going to be able to help them in April. That was an enormous disappointment for me, since I wanted very badly to create a good first impression and to justify Hart's faith in me.

But I also learned my lesson about asking more from my arm than it could possibly give. I spent nearly a month on the disabled list, all the while wondering what it'd take to have one full season without pain. Instead, I went through another long and tedious rehab, building up my arm with strength-and-conditioning exercises, and then finally heading off to Class AAA Buffalo for a thirty-day rehab assignment.

There's nothing worse for a Major Leaguer than to have to perform at the Class AAA level, because the motivation is nonexistent. I was starting my spring training all over, but facing kids who were hungry for a chance to get to the big leagues. If I'd still been with the Yankees, they would've been less concerned about the way I was throwing, because they knew me. But I was new to the Indians, and when I was struggling at Buffalo, John Hart actually told me he wanted me to kick it into gear and start pitching better.

What Hart didn't know, or perhaps couldn't know, is that I was having the worst time of my life in Buffalo. I was away from my family, stuck in a small hotel room, surrounded by teammates who were strangers to me. All I did was go to the ballpark and then come back to the hotel's barren four walls. Meanwhile the Indians were cruising along in the Central Division—all of which contributed to the worst depression of my professional career.

My state of mind was so dark, my wife Monica asked over the phone one day, "Dwight, why don't you just quit?"

For the first time in my career I didn't have a convincing answer. I missed my kids intensely, and wasn't even sure it was worth being away from them.

"What else do you have to prove?" Monica asked.

Again, she was right: I'd been on the winning side of two World Series, had won the Cy Young Award, Rookie of the Year, been an All-Star and a twenty-game winner. Indeed, what was left?

"Honey, just come home," she said.

I wanted to. I wanted to coach my son's Little League team again. I wanted to enjoy the pleasure of a midsummer barbecue and to take my kids to school on the first day of classes. I wanted to have long, lazy breakfasts with Monica, without having to worry about another two-week road trip coming up. And God knows, I wanted to be able to wake up in the morning and not have to ask the eternal question that consumes every pitcher the moment his eyes open: is my arm okay?

The only reason I didn't retire was the sense of pride I had my own career; I didn't want to go out on the disabled list, nor did I want to let the Indians down. They'd gone out of their way for me, and just as I wanted to make George Steinbrenner look good for helping me in 1996, I wanted John Hart to be able to look his peers in the eyes and know signing Dwight Gooden was the right move.

In retrospect, I'm glad I stuck it out, because the summer of 1998 turned out to be a pretty good one. Even though I lost my first three games, and was only 3–6 through July—and there were rumblings of discontent among Indians fans—I didn't lose a game in the last two months of the season.

We were lucky that no one in the division really pressured us—the White Sox were never a factor—because it gave us the chance to focus on the upcoming play-offs. It was fairly obvious that the Yankees were in the middle of an historic season and that whoever drew them in October would have their hands full.

Ironically, I never got to pitch against the Yankees during the regular season; every time they came into town, or we were in New York, it was someone else's turn in the rotation. That was both good and bad, because, on one hand, I wanted very much to show my old teammates how well I was throwing the ball, especially in the second half. But by not facing the Yankees, there'd be an element of surprise that would work in my favor come play-off time.

It's an old axiom in baseball: when neither a pitcher nor a hitter has faced each other, initially, it's the pitcher who can best take advantage of the situation. And as often as the Yankees had seen me throw in 1996 and 1997, there's still a big difference between observing my stuff and actually standing in the batter's box against it.

Obviously, I was going to need whatever advantage I could find against the Yankees, because they were a powerhouse. Not only did they set the all-time American League record with 114 victories, but in my mind, they ranked up there with some of the greatest teams of all time, including the 1927 Yankees, the 1961 Yankees, and the 1975 Reds.

Power, speed, great pitching . . . you name it, and the Yankees had it. I thought a lot of American League teams stopped believing they could beat the Yankees by midsummer; they more or less conceded the season to them and figured they'd have a better chance in 1999. It happens every so often, that an unbeatable team comes along and blows out the division or the entire league early. In that sense, the '98 Yankees reminded me of the '86 Mets.

But I was glad to be part of the Indians, who were closer than the Yankees had ever been in my two years there. It wasn't uncommon for six or seven of us to go out to dinner together on the road, just like the '86 Mets used to, and I forged particularly close friendships with Jim Thome, our first baseman, Mike Jackson, our late-inning closer, and third baseman Travis Fryman.

I rented a big, beautiful home a few minutes outside the city, and found the more I played in Cleveland, the more I liked the atmosphere. The crowds at Jacobs Field were huge and enthusiastic, and just as loud as the fans at Yankee Stadium. The Indians finished the season drawing 3.467 million fans, second in the American League only to the Orioles, who drew 3.685 million at Camden Yards.

We ended up with eighty-nine wins, finishing nine games ahead of the White Sox in the division. The Yankees and Red Sox both had better records than us, but we knew, come play-off time, anything was possible. I learned that lesson the hard way in 1988, when, as a Met, we lost to an inferior Dodger team.

The only thing holding me back was a hernia I suffered in the middle of the summer—my second in two years. I don't even know the exact moment that I suffered the injury, or why, only that I felt extreme pain along my right side—my push-off leg—anytime I tried to throw by reaching back for something extra on my fastball.

There were many, many instances in the second half when I gave up trying to throw hard and instead concentrated on location. I remember Sandy Alomar asking me, "Doc, you must be hurting pretty bad," because of the pained expression on my face when I was on the mound.

The doctors told me I'd need surgery, sooner or later, and in fact, the tear in my abdominal wall was more severe this time than in 1997. But unlike the first injury, I decided to pitch through it, because I knew an operation would end my season. I was the Indians' hottest pitcher down the stretch and I didn't want to miss the play-offs.

As it turned out, we drew the Red Sox in the Division Series, which everyone considered a blessing because it meant the Texas Rangers would have to face the Yankees. I didn't care one way or another, because to get to the World Series, we'd eventually have to pass through the Bronx. What differences would it make if it was in the division or League Championship Series?

Of course, the Rangers were a good team, and very capable of upsetting the Yankees. But that didn't even come close to happening, as they were wiped out in three straight. The Yankees allowed Texas just one run in 27 innings, further proof that they were the team to beat.

We had our hands full with the Red Sox, in a tough best-of-five series. I started Game Three at Fenway Park, with the series tied at one game apiece. I can't say I'm proud of what happened to me that day, although I can't say it was all my fault, either.

My entire workday lasted just four batters, a mere 22 pitches, and I'm still trying to understand what happened. This much was certain: with a 1–0 count on leadoff hitter Darren Lewis, I threw two pitches that cut the plate in half. I'm not talking about the corners, or the knees, or even getting a piece of the black. Those were perfect strikes, yet home-plate umpire Joe Brinkman called them balls.

Missed calls are part of baseball, and a veteran pitcher will accept that. He knows that yelling at the umpire, or rolling the eyes or gesturing in any way can only further aggravate an ump, and in the long run, you pay a price. So while I disagreed strongly with Brinkman, I was careful not to show my displeasure. All I did was look at him. Not stare. Not glare. Just look.

For that, Brinkman went crazy. He whipped off his mask and was shouting at me from behind the plate. I had no idea what he was saying, because the crowd noise drowned him out. But Brinkman had lost his composure and I put my hands up toward him, as if to say, "Okay, calm down. Let's just play ball."

I certainly didn't mean to patronize Brinkman with that gesture, but he was so out of control, I feared that he was about to eject me. My manager, Mike Hargrove, came out to the mound to remind me to stay cool, and I told him, "Those pitches were strikes. I have no idea what's going on here."

Having heard that, Hargrove got right in Brinkman's face, and the two argued loudly right at home plate. Within moments Hargrove was thrown out of the game and that set in motion the series of events that led to my own ejection.

With Brinkman's temper fully ignited, I walked both Lewis and John Valentin. I struck out Mo Vaughn, but then surrendered a double to Nomar Garciaparra, the Red Sox's hugely talented shortstop. Lewis scored on the play, but Brinkman exacted his revenge on me by calling Valentin safe, too, as he scored all the way from first base.

There was no question, none whatsoever, that Valentin was out. Brinkman had no excuse for missing that call, since he was in perfect position. Instead, the Red Sox had their second run, and Brinkman looked at me with an expression that said: "That's what you get for arguing."

I could see the brazen look in his eyes. I could see he wanted another fight. I could see he didn't intend to lose, either. What I didn't understand was why Brinkman had engaged me in this war, because I hardly knew him since I'd been in the American League, and we'd never had a problem.

I'd been backing up home plate on the relay from the outfield, and on my way back to the mound, I leaned into Brinkman and said, "Come on, man, get in the game." Those were my only words. By the time I was standing on the rubber, John Hirschbeck, the second-base umpire, approached me and said, "Doc, you're going to have to leave the field."

"Why?" I asked.

"Because you've been ejected. Joe tossed you."

Now it was my turn to lose my temper, because I felt Brinkman had willfully diminished our chances of winning the game—ejecting both the manager and the starting pitcher—in the very first inning. And both ejections were precipitated by calls that Brinkman clearly missed. Overall, it was a bad postseason for umpires from both leagues, although as I said, mistakes are part of human nature, and certainly a factor in any baseball game.

However, there has to be some consideration for how important the play-offs are, and to so casually strip a team of two key weapons tells me some umpires have lost their perspective. Not all. Not most. But just a few. There's a way to keep control of a game without losing your temper or ejecting anyone who looks at you the wrong way.

Lucky for us we ended up getting past the Red Sox and were able to meet the greatest challenge of the season: a best-of-seven showdown with the Yankees. Everyone said they were on a roll straight through the play-offs and that no one could stop them. No question, the Yankees had a tough, balanced lineup with no holes whatsoever. But we had them on the ropes.

The Yankees won Game One, 7–2, as they jumped all over Jaret Wright in the first inning. He gave up five runs before he could even get three outs, which more or less finished us for the night. I don't know if the Yankees were pumped up by talk that Wright was a headhunter—he'd broken second baseman Luis Sojo's wrist with an errant fastball during spring training—but the real reason Jaret struggled is that he just didn't have his normal command.

We started Charlie Nagy in Game Two against David Cone and we shocked the Yankees by beating them, 4–1, in twelve innings. The key play occurred on Travis Fryman's sacrifice bunt with a runner on first in the twelfth inning, with the score tied, 1–1. Tino Martinez was a little slow fielding the ball, and his throw to Chuck Knoblauch hit Travis on the back and rolled toward right field.

Knoblauch, as well as the rest of the Yankees, were sure that Travis was in fair territory in the baseline and should've been called out for interference. But while the Yankees were busy protesting, Enrique Wilson scored all the way from first base, and we ended up with three decisive runs in the twelfth.

We went even further in proving the Yankees were human in Game Three, winning, 6–1. Bartolo Colon outpitched Andy Pettitte, who allowed six runs in 4.2 innings, including four home runs. Suddenly we could see a path to the World Series; it was there in front of us. All we had to do was win Game Four, and the Yankee monolith would've been virtually obliterated.

Game Four was mine. Ever since I lost those two games in the 1986 World Series, I'd been looking for a chance for October redemption and my only wish was that my father was still alive to see me take the mound against the Yankees.

My excitement was diminished, however, knowing that Darryl Strawberry was very, very sick. During the Division Series against Boston, Straw was diagnosed with colon cancer and I nearly dropped the phone when Ray Negron called me in the hotel to tell me.

"They're going to operate on him," Ray said. "They still don't know how serious it is."

I called Darryl at home immediately to tell him I was praying for him, trying my best to remain composed during the conversation.

"Hang in there, Straw. You know I'm there for you," I said.

"I know, Doc. You know I love you," he answered.

I could tell he was scared, really scared, because he didn't want to talk about the cancer or the medical struggles that would follow his surgery. Instead, Straw wanted to concentrate on baseball, trying to joke with me about having to face the Yankees.

"You know we're gonna light you up, Doc," he said. I laughed. Or at least I made a sound that resembled a laugh. The whole time I was thinking about the crazy times Darryl and I had shared over the years, how young and carefree he once was, and whether that contributed to his illness in any way.

Straw had been through so much in his life—drugs, alcohol, the court system, losing his mother to breast cancer in 1996—it was unfair for him to be struck down again. They say God only gives you the burden that you can handle, but this was too much. My heart went out to Darryl, and it took all my willpower not to break down in tears before I hung up the phone.

By the time our League Championship Series began with the Yankees, all of them were wearing Darryl's number 39 stitched to their caps. I was with them in spirit, praying for my friend. Somehow, I know that if I'd won Game Four, Darryl would've been happy for me personally, and I took those good thoughts to the mound.

Trouble was, I was facing a very accomplished and determined opponent in Orlando "El Duque" Hernandez, who shut us down for seven innings. Hernandez, a Cuban refugee and obviously a very brave man, used an extremely huge leg kick and unorthodox delivery to keep our hitters off balance. We managed just three hits off him in seven innings, which created a zero margin of error for me.

I'd spent plenty of time studying the Yankee hitters, from the scouting reports to videotapes to my own memory of them. I would have to throw my best game to hold them down. I wish I could say I was perfect, but I wasn't. In the first inning, I hung a curveball to Paul O'Neill, allowing him to smoke it over the right-field wall and give the Yankees a 1–0 lead.

I cruised through the second and third innings without trouble, but I hit another wall in the fourth, issuing back-to-back walks to O'Neill and Bernie Williams. For some reason, I stopped trying to make quality pitches, replacing them instead with perfect pitches. In other words, I was pitching defensively, and if there's anything I learned about the Yankees, it's that their patience will wear you out. They very rarely would swing at pitches out of the strike zone.

Both O'Neill and Williams ended up scoring in the Yankees' two-run fourth inning, as Chili Davis—who always hit me hard in the National League—hit an opposite-field double. I left the game with two outs in the fifth trailing 3–0—not a bad day's work, but not enough to stop the Yankees. We ended up losing, 4–0, and when David Wells beat us, 5–3, in Game Five, I knew the Yankees would be all but unstoppable in Game Six at home. I was right: they scored six runs against Charlie Nagy in the first three innings, and the Yankees were the American League champs.

We had nothing to be embarrassed about. In fact, the Indians were the only team to defeat the Yankees in October, as they went on to sweep the Padres four straight in the World Series. As for me, I considered 1998 another good and bad year; I pitched well when healthy, but I'm still looking for one last season when I can have a legitimate chance to win twenty games.

Still, if my career were to end today, I have plenty to be thankful for—especially during my second time around. I appreciate the game in a way I never could have in the eighties, having learned that my gifts were indeed that, gifts to be treasured and nourished and protected. If it took a suspension to appreciate that, then I consider it a worthwhile education.

The only piece of unfinished business is the videotape of my no-hitter against Seattle. I promised my dad we'd watch it together the day he came home from the hospital. After all, that was his game, my present to him.

Dan Gooden was the reason I beat the Mariners. It was his faith in me that kept me strong. It was his love that pulled me through.

"When you get back, you and me, we'll go over that game pitch by pitch," I told my dad one day in the hospital. He smiled at me. I knew that would've made him happy. I only wish he could've come home from the hospital, even for one day, so we could relive that game.

But he never made it. He died in St. Joseph's in January 1997. To this day, the tape sits on a shelf in my office, untouched.

## MY TOP FIVE HITTERS:

1. Barry Bonds: Amazingly quick bat. Can hurt you inside, and won't swing at bad pitches.
2. Chili Davis: Especially tough against me in the National League, as a Giant.
3. Tony Gwynn: Impossible to strike him out.

4. Rafael Palmeiro: Like Bonds, very selective and very strong.
5. Ken Griffey Jr: Stands so close to the plate, almost dares you to pitch himself. But he's hard to beat with a fastball.

## MY TOP FIVE PITCHERS:

1. Roger Clemens: A power pitcher who has enough weapons to beat you even without his fastball.
2. Greg Maddux: A magician who just wins and wins. Makes pitching look as easy as sitting in a rocking chair.
3. Tom Glavine: As gifted as Maddux but without the recognition.
4. David Cone: Pedro Martinez, Maddux, and Clemens all rolled into one. A combination of power and finesse and a true gamer.
5. Nolan Ryan: The greatest power pitcher ever.

## MY TOP FIVE TEAMS:

1. The 1998 Yankees: Possibly the best collection of players baseball has ever known.
2. The 1996 Indians: Dangerous lineup, top to bottom.
3. The 1996 Mariners: With Griffey, Alex Rodriguez, Edgar Martinez, and Jay Buhner, a four-headed, pitcher-eating monster.
4. The 1985 Cardinals: A team that was perfectly constructed for AstroTurf, but with enough power, thanks to Jack Clark, to make them dangerous, too.
5. The 1993 Phillies: From last place in 1992, all the way to the World Series a year later. They took down a tremendous Braves team to win the National League pennant.

## MY TOP FIVE PITCHING MOUNDS:

1. Dodger Stadium: Perfectly manicured; you feel like you're right on top of the hitter.
2. Yankee Stadium: Love those huge dimensions in the gaps. Very pitcher-friendly.
3. Shea Stadium: Good dimensions there, too.
4. Jacobs Field: A perfect, steep tilt to the mound. The drop-off is severe, just the way I like it.
5. Astrodome: Another place where I feel very, very close to the hitter.

# I N D E X

Roycemore School
MS/US Library
640 Lincoln Street
Evanston, IL 60201